Playing Pasts

Edited by Dave Day

A *Playing Pasts* **Sports and Leisure History Magazine Publication**

Playing Pasts Edited by Dave Day

First published March 2020 by
Playing Pasts Online Sports and Leisure History Magazine
Geoffrey Manton 0-14.
Rosamund Street West
Manchester
M15 6EB

Website: http://www.playingpasts.co.uk/
Twitter: @Playing_Pasts

ISBN paperback 978-1-910029-56-5

Available from
http://buyonline.mmu.ac.uk/browse/product.asp?catid=67&modid=1&compid=1

Printed and bound in Great Britain by Manchester Metropolitan University

Front Cover: Cheshire County Training College Hockey Team, 1914-15.
Courtesy of the Sport and Leisure History Research Archive, MMU Cheshire.

Table of Contents

Acknowledgement.
Playing Pasts would like to thank Manchester Metropolitan University History Research Centre for the funding that enabled this volume to be printed.

Introduction

The digital era is changing history as it has been understood and practiced involving a shift in the traditional ontological, epistemological and methodological thinking that privileges the academic historian over public historians and academic histories over public histories. Digital technologies and platforms have accelerated the involvement of the public both as researchers and creators of histories who make their own meanings about the past without the mediation of professional historians. This popularization of history as practice and pursuit challenges the traditional separation between the distant and recent past. It also emphasizes that we need to regard history as something living, ongoing, and dynamic rather than quarantined to the past. For the sports and leisure historian, seeing history through this lens can broaden and change methodological practice.[1]

In response to these changes in the environment, Manchester Metropolitan University's Sport and Leisure History (SpLeisH) research team hosted a seminar on the topic of the future for sports history as a sub-discipline of history in June 2015. This brought together academics involved in researching and teaching sport and leisure history with non-academic researchers and sporting heritage practitioners to reflect on the status of the field. The consensus was that the sports history community needed to do something different and this was reinforced the following year with the publication of a special issue of *The International Journal of the History of Sport* on methodologies, subsequently published as a book, [2] which explored the range of research tools and approaches now available to sports and leisure historians. This stimulated further thinking about ways in which research could be disseminated more widely and how the field could be extended to include both academic and non-academic interest groups. The online sports and leisure history magazine *Playing Pasts* (www.playingpasts.co.uk) emerged as a result.

Playing Pasts was launched in September 2016 to provide a platform for all sports and leisure history constituencies. As a free to access online magazine it was designed to make more widely available the research findings of British and International colleagues, most of which was being published in academic journals not easily available to the

---

[1] Gary Osmond and Murray G. Phillips (eds) *Sport History in the Digital Era.* (University of Illinois, 2015), 24-25.

[2] Dave Day and Wray Vamplew, (eds) *Methodology in Sports History.* (London: Routledge, 2017).

extensive worldwide community interested in the subject area. In addition, since a substantial proportion of the international sports history community operates outside of academia, the magazine was structured to engage independent, non-academic researchers and facilitate their activities through extending their networks and providing an outlet for their work. Further motivations for introducing *Playing Pasts* as an online magazine included the recognition within the SpLeisH research group of the urgent need to develop a higher status for this field of research and to enthuse and educate others about this area of history. In particular, the editorial team were keen to make visible issues surrounding gender and minorities in sport, as well as exposing hidden histories around place and identity. The overall aim was to generate a truly collaborative arena, widening knowledge through different networks of the importance of local histories, identifying lost individuals and communities, and connecting with international researchers and interest groups.

Thanks primarily to the time and effort invested by the Editor-in-Chief, Margaret Roberts, who has been in charge of its content since its inception, *Playing Pasts* now provides a unique opportunity for established scholars, early-career researchers, postgraduates, and non-academic practitioners from around the world to publicize their work in an accessible and visually arresting blog format, which appeals to communities that are often disconnected from Higher Education research agendas. Although there are a number of academic journals dedicated to the area, *Playing Pasts* is different in that it aims to present historical material related to sport and leisure in a widely readable and accessible format. The magazine is presented solely as an online publication and, while the main articles are invariably based on rigorous and traditional scholarly research, the material has been presented in shortened form and accompanied by numerous illustrations to allow the reader to explore and engage with a range of different ideas and research. The magazine is also different from other publications in that it is not divided into discrete issues, but material is added on a weekly basis, so there is always something fresh and new, while existing material is archived for easy reader access. Contributions are welcomed from anyone who feels they have something they would like to share about the history of sport and leisure, which is interpreted as widely as possible in this context, whether that be circuses or pantomime, fell walking or climbing, unusual or traditional sports, or anything else that historians have a passion about.

During the magazine's first year, over 40 individuals from different scholarly constituencies showcased their research. Since then, the site has expanded rapidly and now 88 different authors have contributed, including 31 academics, 42 non-academics, 10 postgraduates, and 5 early-career researchers. The total access to date amounts to over 460,00, the site is now attracting over 21,000 reads per month, and the *Playing Pasts* twitter account currently has over 1,100 followers. Magazine content has included popular digests, such as 'On this week in Sport and Leisure History' and 'Where Are They Now?', which have been augmented by sections devoted to podcasts and videoed lectures. Further sections will be added over the course of the next few years in response to emerging areas of interest to sports and leisure historians.

The site is truly innovative: before its inception there was no global digital outlet for the public history of sports and leisure. *Playing Pasts* has not only allowed intellectual exchange between academic and public historians to thrive, it has also brought their work to new audiences, enabled democratic commentary and engagement through social media, and increased the credibility of the subject by highlighting its popularity within communities around the world. The magazine's international reach is highlighted by the nationalities of those involved in contributing (including France, Belgium, Poland, Netherlands, Denmark, Canada, America, Italy, Serbia, Spain, Japan, Mexico, Australia, and Ireland) and by reading/viewing figures, which place the US (136,275), France (39,372), Germany (33,301), China (26,812), and Sweden (11,408) as the top five non-UK countries engaging with the site. Recent reader comments include: 'As someone who, from birth, has never been interested in sport, I am constantly amazed at how many articles in *Playing Pasts* I find totally absorbing' (retired librarian), and 'Currently enjoying *Playing Pasts*. Journals without pictures are like fish without chips so I always look forward to its arrival' (emeritus professor).

A *Playing Pasts* forum held in March 2019 provided an opportunity to bring together contributors to the magazine from different sports and leisure communities to showcase their work, to discuss the benefits of publishing in the online magazine, and to share ideas about the future direction of the magazine. In addition to podcasting their presentations, several attendees expressed a desire to write something more substantial and the content of this volume reflects the results of their efforts. The contributors to this volume reflect the diverse nature of the *Playing Pasts* community with chapters from leading academics (Huggins), early career academics (Heffernan, Harris and Garcia), doctoral students (Martin), and independent researchers from the UK (Roberts, Webb, Evans and Fishpool) and Europe (Bonini and Walenta). Similarly, the topics covered give a flavour of the breadth of papers presented on *Playing Pasts*, as short papers, podcasts and videos. Mike Huggins addresses a long-neglected period in the history of sport and one that deserves much more attention while new perspectives are brought to bear on the history of women's sport with chapters on cycling by Mike Fishpool, athletics by Derek Martin, and hockey Mark Evans. The international history of sport is illustrated by Gherardo Bonini in his biography of Otto Herschmann, Carlos Garcia's reflection on the 1992 Barcelona Olympics, and Filip Walenta's discussion of cycling in Belgium during the Great War. The remaining three chapters address some of the 'hidden histories' that would remain uncovered were it not for the enthusiasm and diligence of enthusiastic researchers. Conor Heffernan addresses the development of Irish bodybuilding, Margaret Roberts and Sarah Webb explore student sport in the Edwardian period, and Luke Harris presents a biography of Jack Price, who ran in the 1908 Olympic Marathon.

It is hoped that readers will enjoy the eclectic nature of this volume and that they might, in turn, feel motivated to make their own contribution at some point in the future. All they have to do is contact Margaret Roberts at *Playing Pasts* (www.playingpasts.co.uk @playing_pasts).

Notes on Contributors

Mike Huggins moved into university teaching as an historian after completing his doctorate at Lancaster University. His first book, *Flat Racing and British Society 1790-1914* (Routledge), won the prestigious NASSH book award in 2000. He is now an emeritus professor of cultural history at the University of Cumbria. He has singly or jointly produced many books and edited collections and over a hundred book chapters and academic articles. His research interests encompass sports history in Britain over the past three centuries, most recently developing interests in the long eighteenth century; sport and visuality; sport, gambling and match-fixing; and the history of horse racing. His most recent monograph is *Horse Racing and British Society in the Long Eighteenth Century* (Boydell, 2018). His edited collection *A Cultural History of Sport in the Age of Industry* (Bloomsbury) comes out in 2020. He is on the editorial boards of five sports history journals. He is a Fellow of the Royal Historical Society, a Fellow of the European Committee for Sports History, and a Fellow of the British Society for Sports History. He is currently President of the European Committee for Sports History.

Conor Heffernan is Assistant Professor of Physical Culture and Sport Studies at the University of Texas at Austin. In 2019 he completed his PhD. at University College Dublin on the Irish physical culture movement from 1890 to 1939. A specified health movement concerned with the cultivation of the body, physical culture permeated across social, economic, political and sexual lives in Ireland. It is for this reason that issues of agency, identity formation and gender politics lie at the heart of the research. In the past, Conor has published on sport and identity in post- colonial Africa, the transnational history of Indian club swinging in Victorian England, physical culture commerce in Ireland and, most recently, the possibilities offered by animal history to sporting historians. Additionally, for the past four years Conor has operated as editor and contributor to physicalculturestudy.com, an online website whose sole focus is the history of physical culture and health trends more generally. Designed as a platform for his present research into Irish physical culture, the website covers a variety of decades and regions in its discussion of physical culture.

Margaret Roberts is a highly experienced and well-respected genealogist and, as a research associate with the ManMet Sport and Leisure History Research Team also works with academics, researchers, PhD students and families both at home and abroad to help uncover many forms of sporting past. She is currently employed as a research assistant at ManMet, she is the long-term Editor-in-Chief of *Playing Pasts* and she curated the Sport and Leisure History Archive at MMU Cheshire. Margaret is an organizing member of the Family History Society of Cheshire and a well-known local speaker, delivering talks on a wide range of subjects from family history to female sport. Margaret has recently published *Swimming Communities in Victorian England* (2019), and From Butlins to Europe: Fodens Ladies in the 1960s and 1970s (*Sport in History*, 2019), both co-authored with Dave Day. Currently, she is continuing her research into Fodens Ladies football team as well as working with Sarah Webb on the history of teaching training in Cheshire, focussing in particular on the female staff and students of the Cheshire County Training College in Crewe.

Sarah Webb is an assistant librarian at Manchester Metropolitan University. She has been a volunteer at Tabley House, Cheshire (University of Manchester) since 2004 and was appointed as a trustee of the Tabley House Collection in 2009. She was awarded the Stephen Matthews prize for history writing in 2012 for her article in *Cheshire History* about Tabley Old Hall. Her Masters dissertation on aspects of the Tabely House library was published as 'Sir Francis Leicester's "Good Library" at Nether Tabley' in *Library & Information*

History, XXXIV, issue 1, 2018. She is the editor of *The Friends of Tabley Newsletter* commissioning new research on the collection and its archive (Cheshire Archives and Local Studies and The John Rylands Library, University of Manchester) twice a year. In 2018, she co-curated the exhibition *Women Educating Cheshire* with Margaret Roberts for ManMet's Cheshire campus at Crewe (funded by The Sylvia Pankhurst Gender and Diversity Research Centre). With her co-author Margaret Roberts she published in 2019 'A Library in Green Fields: A History of the Cheshire County Training College, Crewe and later Manchester Metropolitan University Cheshire Campus Library Service', *Cheshire History*, 59.

Mike Fishpool has spent over two decades working in publishing and writing roles and graduated from Aberystwyth University in the 1990s after reading international politics. He has since studied at Birkbeck, University of London, gaining an MA in Historical Research in 2017. His dissertation looked at the attitudes towards women's cycle racing and its brief rise in the UK, France and the United States during the late nineteenth Century. Since completing his MA, Mike has written various papers on early women's cycling history for the *Playing Pasts* website, comprising 'Lady Racers: The Origins of Women's Cycle Racing', 'Miles and Laps: Women's Cycle Racing in Great Britain at the turn of the 19th Century' and 'Mrs Grace versus Lisette: A comparison of the English and French Women's Cycling Champions'. He additionally produced an illustrated article entitled 'Lisette - France's Most Popular Lady Racer' that was published in the Veteran-Cycle Club's journal *The Boneshaker* in Winter 2018, providing the first detailed biography on the French rider. Mike also participates in a women's cycling history group that brings together several leading academics, researchers and writers to collaborate and share their research on the subject.

Luke Harris is an Honorary Research Fellow in the Department of History at the University of Birmingham. His main interest lies in Britain's Olympic History, along with a focus on the history of sport in Birmingham. He is currently in the process of writing a biography of the Edwardian distance runner, Jack Price.

Gherardo Bonini (1959) has been working from 1989 at the Historical Archives of European Union (HAEU) in Florence, since 2013 as Deputy Director. He learnt the methodology of sport science from 1990 to 1995 when Professor Pierre Lanfranchi was teaching history of sport in the European University Institute (EUI), to which HAEU is attached. He joined the European Committee for Sports History (CESH) in 1999, he co-founded the Italian section of CESH in 2004, and became a member of the International Society of History and Physical Education and Sports (ISHPES) in 2015. He has written short contributions for *Encyclopedia of World Sport* (1996), *International Encyclopedia of Women Sport* (2001), *Encyclopedia of British Sport* (2000), *Encyclopedia of British Football* (2002), and *Berkshire's Encyclopedia of World Sport* (2005). Gherardo has collaborated from 2000 to 2016 to *Milo. The Journal of Serious Strength Sports*, publishing more than 30 articles. With Franco Cervellati, he co-authored two monographs *Fiorentini in acqua d'Arno* (2004) on swimming, and *Giuseppe Cassioli. L'artista delle medaglie* (2019) about the artist who modeled the effigies of Olympic medal in force from 1928 to 2000. Gherardo's main interest changed from his initial investigation about weightlifting's and swimming's history and now he focuses on Austrian sport in Interwar and immediate Post-war period.

Carlos García-Martí is a lecturer at the Universidad Europea de Madrid, teaching Sport History and Sport Sociology at the Faculty of Sports Sciences. Graduated in Sociology, he conducted his PhD in Sport Sciences at the Universidad Politécnica de Madrid. His research focus is on sport and national identities and professional sport cultures. He has written about changing football styles in Spain and its relationship with national identity during the Francoist regime and during democracy. He has studied how tactical modifications can collide with political ideologies or accompany social changes. In the Spanish case, he has studied how the traditional *Fury* style was substituted after the 80's by the elegant *tiki-taka*, reflecting more profound social changes. He has also studied how the Spanish media has treated the doping phenomenon and the conflictual interpretations registered during the years previous to the 1992 Olympic Games. He is currently working on the history of training, physical culture and coaching in Spain and the professionalization of football players during the transition to democracy. He has published both in English and Spanish and is a member of the Spanish Association of Social Sciences Research in Sport (AEISAD) and the Spanish Federation of Sociology (FES).

Mark Evans is a retired police officer who has an interest in the history of all sports, particularly hockey, athletics, swimming, water polo and sport in Manchester. Prior to joining the Police, he attended Keele University, obtaining a degree in Geography and Geology. Since retirement. Mark has become a volunteer with the Hockey Museum. He has conducted research for the Museum on ladies league hockey, the history of the English Ladies Hockey Leagues Association. and the history of both the Mitton Challenge Shield and the English Cup. He is currently continuing his research into ladies league hockey in the North during the early part of the twentieth century. He has written articles for the online sports forum 'Playing Pasts' and attended a number of sports conferences. He is a member of the British Society of Sports History and Sporting Heritage. He is a life member of Trafford Athletic Club and vice chair at Radcliffe Swimming and Water Polo where he also coaches swimming. He is still active in a number of sports. His son plays hockey for Surbiton Hockey Club and his daughter plays for Leicester Hockey Club. His daughter-in-law is currently an England and Great Britain international hockey player.

Derek Martin is a qualified lawyer and latterly a Principal Lecturer in Law at Leeds Beckett University. He is now a doctoral candidate at Manchester Metropolitan University, researching the history of athletics in the seventeenth, eighteenth and nineteenth centuries. He has published book chapters and delivered several conference papers on the origins and early development of the sport. Having been an ultra-distance runner of very modest attainment until his knees gave way, he has a particular interest in recovering the biographies of the long-distance runners and walkers who were a significant but neglected (and in the case of the women, an almost totally forgotten) part of 'pedestrianism'.

Filip Walenta is a former competitive triathlete and cyclist, living in Ghent (Belgium). Professionally, he is a meteorologist and currently working as a senior weather forecaster in the Belgian Air Force for the Search and Rescue (SAR) helicopters at the Belgian coast. As a committee member for about fifteen years, and three years as president, of his cycling club Filip founded Karelvanwijnendaele.be, a digital historical research project about the life of Karel Van Wijnendaele, editor-in-chief of the Flemish leading sports magazine *Sportwereld* in the beginning of the twentieth century and organizer of the Tour of Flanders. His research interest lies in the history of competitive cycling and sports journalism in the nineteenth and early twentieth century in Belgium. As a member of the historical organization Ghent-on-Files, connected to the Ghent City archive, he regularly contributes articles on sports history of the city. In order to obtain better historical insights and to learn the right skills for historical research he started his studies in cultural history at the Open University of Heerlen in the Netherlands in 2018.

Proto-modernity and Sport in Britain

Mike Huggins

Abstract
This chapter reviews and challenges some of the generally accepted assumptions about the relationship between sport and modernization during the long eighteenth century. It argues that many of the structural features of modern sport were already appearing, albeit in rather different form. It reviews the strengths and weaknesses of current historiography, and some of the problems of recent research, suggesting that they have contributed to misunderstandings in secondary works. It presents 'proto-modern sport' as a time during which the conditions for modern sport emerged: these included the development of a more commercialized sporting culture from quite early on; rapid population growth over the period; the expansion of provincial newspaper coverage; the expansion of the toll-road system; the all-pervasive wagering on sporting events such as horseracing, cricket, pugilism or cock-fighting; formal and informal associativity; and the emergence of a leisure class amongst the titled and gentry.

Keywords: Early Modern: Proto-modernity; Gambling; Associativity; Commercialization.

Introduction
The recent assertions of a 'proto-modern' phase of British sporting development, dating from c.1660s to the mid-nineteenth century, are beginning to problematize what have often been seen as the apparently rigid historical boundaries drawn between 'modern' and 'pre-modern' sports. This proto-modern phase can be defined as a gradual evolution of thought and socio-cultural atmosphere, during which sports adapted to changing historical contexts, preceding and paving the way for modern sport. It can be argued that the changes which took place during this period were crucial in creating 'modern' sport, and that modern sport was thus in its origins a Georgian rather than a Victorian phenomenon. This approach offers a way of opening up a rather different perspective on development in early modern Britain, a period when a new world of commercialized leisure emerged and sports like horse racing, boxing and cricket became serious components of Georgian social practices. Whilst there was still much participative more

casual sporting play to be found, the emphasis was increasingly moving towards more organized physical activities, using more standardized rules, giving entertainment to spectators, often encouraging widespread gambling, and using (semi)professional players. Sporting culture had increased elements of commonality but was still differentiated by local, regional and sport-specific variations.

Sport and modernization

For the last three decades the emphasis in Anglophone historiography has been on the key concept of sporting 'modernization', often linked implicitly to an apparent expansion in the regularity of mass spectator sport. A series of scholars, including Elias, Dunning, Stockvis, Guttmann, Eichberg, Darbon and Vamplew have all explored this movement towards so-called 'modernization' over past centuries in some detail, albeit adopting a variety of theoretical approaches. They all contrasted 'modern sport' with earlier forms, and attempted to identify its key characteristics, although such approaches have been inclined to ignore regional developments and skated over specific historical contexts. They claimed that while such characteristics also appeared sporadically in earlier periods, in 'modernity' these characteristics interacted systematically, in widespread ways.[1]

Norbert Elias, and subsequent followers like Eric Dunning, argued for the 'sportization' of cultural activities and games through the development of codes of conduct and rules, and changing attitudes to the amount of violence acceptable.[2] Dunning and Ken Sheard, for example, showed fifteen ways older folk games contrasted with modern sport.[3] Guttmann emphasized the rational 'sportification' of physical culture.[4] This chronology of increased overall standardization of sports, allowed comparisons to be made, varied from place to place and from sport to sport, as sports began to develop and increasingly link together their key elements. Using a Weberian model, Guttmann argued that the formal-structural characteristics of modern sport were secularism, specialization, bureaucratization, rationalization, quantification,

---

[1] Allen Guttmann, *From Ritual to Record: The Nature of Modern Sport* (New York: Columbia University Press, 1978),172.

[2] Norbert Elias and Eric Dunning (eds.), *Sport and Leisure in the Civilizing Process* (Oxford: Basil Blackwell, 1986).

[3] Eric Dunning and Ken Sheard, *Barbarians, Gentlemen and Players: A Sociological Study of Rugby Football* (Oxford: Martin Robertson, 1979).

[4] Guttmann, *From Ritual to Record*; Richard Guilianotti, *Sport: A Critical Sociology* (London: Polity Press, 2005).

equality, and obsession with records. [5] Stockvis emphasized the international organization and control of sports as key. [6] Henning Eichberg likewise implied that sport's emergence was part of broader modernization processes.[7] In 2014, Sebastien Darbon suggested there needed to be more stress on specific sporting spaces and the role of precise timings.[8] Joyce Kay and Wray Vamplew critiqued Guttmann's approach and emphasized other factors including the availability of public information, professionalism and commercialization.[9]

Clearly, 'modernity' is a complex term. It has widely varied meanings and trajectories in every society. It is a contrast concept, taking its meanings from what it denies as much as what it affirms [10] Many sociological and historical texts still over-simply by contrasting 'modern' sport with what are described as 'traditional' or 'pre-modern' sports. Such terms are loose and problematic. All sporting traditions have to be invented and reinvented. Moreover, when does modernity actually begin? After all, every society in the past has thought of itself as modern. The criteria above were all ideal-type postulations. Even late-nineteenth-century individual sports rarely fulfilled all the criteria.

Even so, there has been a broad consensus amongst historians of sport that the middle years of the nineteenth century saw the emergence of a more recognizably modern, more achievement-oriented and commercial sporting culture. Though the chronology of these changes has been debated, and historical approaches should really adopt a rather more sceptical approach to chronology, change and continuity, generally it has been this mid-nineteenth time which arguably saw 'the birth of modern sport' or a global sporting 'revolution'. Tranter describes the period as showing 'a notable transformation in the scale

---

[5] Guttmann, *From Ritual to Record*; Allen Guttmann, *Sports: The First Five Millenia* (Amherst: University of Massachusetts Press, 2004), 4-5.

[6] R. Stockvis, 'Sport and Civilisation: Is Violence the Central Problem', in *Sport and Leisure in the Civilising Process* ed. Eric Dunning and Chris Rojek (Basingstoke: Macmillan, 1992), 134.

[7] See Susan Brownell, 'Thinking Dangerously: The Person and his Ideas', in *Body Cultures: Essays on Sport, Space and Identity*, ed. Henning Eichberg (London: Routledge, 1998), 28-9.

[8] Sebastian Darbon, *Les Fondements du Systeme Sportif* (Paris: L'Harmattan, 2014).

[9] Joyce Kay and Wray Vamplew, 'A Modern Sport? 'From Ritual to Record' in British Horseracing', *Ludica* 9 (2003): 125-129.

[10] Krishnan Kumar, *The Rise of Modern Society: Aspects of the Social and Political Development of the West* (London: Blackwell, 1988); Jim McGuigan, *Modernity and Post-modern Culture* (Maidenhead: Open University Press, 2006).

and nature of Britain's sporting culture'.[11] This was when, claimed Peter Borsay, 'industrialization and urbanization bite so deeply that they stimulated a quantitative and qualitative change in leisure *En masse*, penetrating most regions and social classes'.[12]

The most significant feature of this change, often underemphasized by historians, was the quantitative shift that then appeared in the regularity, *frequency* and published calendars of contests as growing wealth and free time allowed spectator numbers to rise, encouraging a more consistently commercial approach. By contrast in the eighteenth century, commercialized contests were fewer, and in most towns usually relatively rare events each year, to be saved up for, to watch and to wager on, and to enjoy their ancillary attractions. There was insufficient money for such leisure available in the accessible region round about for this to be more regular. Many sporting events attracting spectators, such as rowing, pedestrianism, pugilism, or local football contests were often annual events, and very few towns had more than one annual race meeting.

London was an exception, a sporting market unique in terms of size, complexity, affluence and compactness, pioneering the longer-term trend towards the commercialization of sporting leisure, as other towns increasing aped its events and fashions. But even here, for cricket, probably the most regularly scheduled London event, between 1730 and 1773 there were only around five matches reported annually at London's Artillery ground, and at Lord's ground in 1787 only eight matches were played. Its cultural satellites, Epsom, Barnet, Egham, Ascot, Hampstead and Hounslow, all occasionally supported single annual race meetings.[13]

So, what *was* happening back in the long-eighteenth century? Here we still understand much less than we should, although our understanding is being slowly changed by revisionist new findings and discoveries. What is clear from work done so far on specific sports in the long eighteenth century is that many of the structural features of modern sport were already appearing, albeit in rather different form. In the case

---

[11] Neil Tranter, S*port, Economy and Society in Modern Britain 1750-1914* (Cambridge: Cambridge University Press, 1997), 13. Dennis Brailsford, *Sport, Time and Society: The British at Play* (Abingdon: Routledge, 2014), 65 saw it as starting in the 1870s.

[12] Peter Borsay, *A History of Leisure* (Basingstoke: Palgrave, 2006).

[13] Mike Huggins, *Horse Racing and British Society in the Long Eighteenth Century* (Woodbridge: Boydell, 2018), 69.

of the gambling-linked sport of horse-racing, to take just one example, local races were bureaucratized and run by race committees and clerks of the course; they were totally secular; based on the specialist skills of judges, jockeys and trainers; run by rules with large elements of commonality; with races often timed by interested individuals, and records of results kept. Attempts to maintain equality of competition through devices like handicapping and weight for height or age were also common.[14] Likewise, Conrad Brustrom and Tanya Cassidy argue that 'by the 1780s cricket resembled the modern game in many key particulars'.[15]

Current historiography: a brief review
The complex intersections between sports and the multiple cultural, social, religious, economic and political contexts in which they were set within English society during the long eighteenth century have remained largely underexplored. A substantial body of detailed research is only slowly beginning to emerge. In recent years, most historians of sport have shown relatively little interest in those eras before the nineteenth century. The history of the early modern has attracted only a relative handful of researchers. This provides a stark comparison with the depth of research on the nineteenth and twentieth centuries.

Of the more substantive works available, some authors offered general overviews of sport during the early modern period that were rather more top-down in their approach, although also exploring popular amusements. There was a tendency to emphasize sport's role in encouraging forms of associativity and social integration, sometimes within a class, and sometimes between classes. Dennis Brailsford *Sport and Society: Elizabeth to Anne* (London: Toronto: University of Toronto Press), in 1969 was stronger on the Tudor and Puritan phases than on the period from 1660 onwards. Brailsford largely focused on attitudes towards sport and exercise, and the relationship between social and intellectual movements and their impact on sport. His later works such as *A Taste for Diversions: Sport in Georgian England* (London: James Clark 1999) offered more thematic surveys and deepened our knowledge of

---

[14] See Huggins, *Horse Racing and British Society*; Joyce Kay and Wray Vamplew,' A Modern Sport? From Ritual to Record in British Horseracing', *Ludica* 9 (2003): 125-139.
[15] Conrad Brustrom and Tanya Cassidy, 'Scorn Eunuch Sports': Class, Gender and the Context of Early Cricket', *Journal for Eighteenth-Century Studies* 35 no. 2 (2012): 226.

early modern sport.[16] T.S Hendrick's *Disputed Pleasures: Sport and Society in Pre-industrial England* (London: Greenwood Press, 1991), a functionalist approach to sporting life from 1066 onwards, includes only a chapter on Georgian sport, emphasizing sports' twin role in reinforcing class and status divisions and providing a mechanism for social integration.

Derek Birley's *Sport and the Making of Britain* (Manchester: Manchester University Press, 1993) included four chapters covering the period from 1603 to 1815. An idiosyncratic approach, almost entirely based on secondary reading, linking sport to the changing social and political scene, it offered limited new insights. It mainly emphasized the influence of the social and economic elite and was not always critically well received.[17]

Robert Malcolmson's book *Popular Recreations in English Society*, 1700-1850 (Cambridge: Cambridge University Press, 1973) was long seen as the definitive study of eighteenth-century popular recreation. Adopting a cultural materialist Marxist approach, he argued that prior to the late eighteenth century, the labouring people of England enjoyed a rich, vital recreational sporting culture of athletic contests, ball games, games of skill and chance, animal sports and combat sports that was enmeshed with and derived its meaning from the economic and social patterns of rural, localized life. He suggested that these relationships then waned thanks to a combination of moral earnestness, social reform and industrial capitalism.

Richard Holt's *Sport and the British* (Clarendon Press, Oxford 1989), clearly influenced by Elias's work, described the early modern period as demonstrating 'old ways of playing' what he termed 'traditional sports' though he accepted that the time was one of changes as well as continuities. His coverage was relatively cursory (pp.12-28) and largely based on the very limited secondary sources then available, so it needs revision in the light of more recent work. His study contained significant numbers of inaccuracies, exaggerating the power of those bodies like the MCC and Jockey Club, whose influence was then *highly* geographically limited and sporadic, and suggesting that sports like bull-baiting and cock-fighting were 'very common' whereas both were

---

[16] Dennis Brailsford, *British Sport: A Social History* (Cambridge: Lutterworth Press, 1992); Brailsford *Sport, Time and Society*.
[17] See for example J. K. Walton, *The English Historical Review*, CXI, no. 44 (1996): 556; Wray Vamplew, *History* 80, no. 258 (1995): 156-7.

already becoming regionally confined even in the second half of the eighteenth century.

Emma Griffin's *England's Revelry: A History of Popular Sports and Pastimes, 1660-1830* (Oxford: Oxford University Press, 2005) was largely a study of the leisure of the common people, with its sporting focus predominantly focusing on the ways bullbaiting in the West Midlands came under challenge, together with some material on control of urban streets more generally and leisure in West Yorkshire, focusing particularly on contexts of space and power.

Though there are several scholarly articles on specific sports, too many to discuss here,[18] there are still only two sports that have received monograph-length attention: on cricket and horse-racing. Both had social elite involvement but dealt with the sports in cross-class ways. David Underdown, *Start of Play: Cricket and Culture in 18th-Century England* (London: Allen Lane, 2000), traced the origins of cricket in the south-east, its growing cross-class popularity, and the growth of clubs such as Hambledon and the MCC. He linked its growth to rural economic life and culture, aristocratic leisure and habits of political deference. More recently Mike Huggins in *Horse Racing and British Society in the Long Eighteenth Century* (Woodbridge: Boydell, 2018) explored race meetings, links with politics and gambling, rules and the running of meetings, the thoroughbred and breeding, and the professionalized world of jockeys, trainers and stable hands.

Edited collections are also now beginning to emerge. Sharon Harrow's British *Sporting Life and Culture in the Long Eighteenth Century* (Farnham: Ashgate, 2015) covered a range of topics including recreational games, clothing, archery, tennis, celebrity, and boxing. Rebekka von Mallinckrodt and Angela Schattner *Sports and Physical Exercise in Early Modern Culture: New Perspectives on the History of Sports and Motion* (London: Routledge 2016) focused mainly on the period before 1700 and on early-modern Europe more broadly, covering British pugilism, sports venues, and competitive and non-competitive forms of sport, physical training and games.

Some of the problems of existing research
Conventional sports history chronology has proposed a picture of a shift from 'traditional' sporting life as it came under increasing attack in the

---

[18] For a recent example see Mike Huggins, Early Modern Sport' in *The Oxford Handbook of Sport History,* ed. Robert Edelman and Wayne Wilson (Oxford: Oxford University Press, 2017): 113-127

eighteenth and early nineteenth century, supposedly accompanying the Industrial Revolution.[19] This led Richard Holt in 1989 to stress what he called 'old ways of playing' and 'traditional games' as characterizing British sport right up to the early nineteenth century, when these attacks had succeeded. In this prior period the research stress was often on agrarian, village, religion-linked sporting activities, supported tacitly by the elite.

Fig. 1. Brighton Races.

Existing studies rightly demonstrated from contemporary published texts that there was opposition to sports of many kinds from middle-class social reformers and more puritanically inclined individuals. This material offered critical arguments about cruel sports. It pointed out that sports were associated with gambling and drinking, which could have adverse effects. They stressed that sports wasted time that could be devoted to productive work. But such testimony cannot be taken at face value, engaged as it was in cultural discourse and assertions of ideological identity. Such opposition, as with that concerning wakes and fairs, was most vociferous when events took place in town centres, with large crowds generating rowdiness and criminality and

---

[19] Robert Malcolmson, *Popular Recreations in English Society 1700-1850* (Cambridge, Cambridge University Press, 1973).

constraining local businesses and free passage. And the animal cruelty surrounding urban bull running and baiting was visible, unlike that of hunting where it remained largely unseen. Where historiography has been weak is that there has been insufficient recognition of the extent to which such literary critiques were those of a minority with often limited power to change wider attitudes. It was contested, challenged or simply ignored.

More recently there has been increased challenge to the conventional view that industrializing Britain over the long eighteenth century witnessed a sharp increase in the volume and intensity of elite criticism of working-class sports and pastimes. Griffin, for example, now suggests that while there was some ambivalence towards sport, there was a substantial degree of toleration. Many were indifferent and though there were some hostile voices, 'the majority thought some measure of regulated diversion was to be encouraged' so the idea of a' decisive shift in attitudes towards traditional pastimes of the poor does not appear to be so well grounded as has long been assumed'.[20]

Existing research, especially that written from the 1970s until the late 1990s, has also distorted understandings by its common focus on what Elias and Dunning called 'folk games', and sports like folk football, rather than on any broader view of sport. Concentration on theories of the 'civilizing process' and the related issues of violence and social control have distracted historians of sport from wider issues. Change factors are more complex than that. Historical change in sport is a process with no clear fixed starting points, and there is general acceptance by sociologists that it is 'uneven and prone to reversals'.[21] Sporting changes in Britain need to be related to multiple variables, to urban and rural sport; to regional differences, as in the different forms of wrestling in Cumbria or Cornwall, or the relatively greater success of cricket in southern England; to the degree of male and female participation (gender issues were neglected by Elias), or to social class as in sports like fox-hunting. The rise and fall of particular sports can be related to broader social attitudes, as in the case of cockfighting, or to mere fashion. Archery, for example, was popular in the 1660s, and then

---

[20] Emma Griffin, 'Wholesome Recreations and Cheering influences. Popular Recreations and Social Elites in Eighteenth Century Britain' in *British Sporting Literature and Culture in the Long Eighteenth Century ed.* Sharon Harrow (Farnham: Ashgate, 2015), 19-34.

[21] Patrick Murphy, Ken Sheard and Ivan Waddington, 'Figurational Sociology and its Application to Sport', in *The Handbook of Sports Studies* ed. J. J. Coakley and Eric Dunning (London: Sage, 2000), 104.

declined, with a few rural societies appearing only briefly, but then revived in the 1770s.

Individual sports have their own lifecycle, sometimes unrelated to broader leisure patterns. So, change in sport has often been an unhurried and gradual transition, with large elements of continuity. In his 1998 study, Neil Tranter showed clearly that there are usually uneven patterns of change and significant elements of continuity with earlier forms of sport.[22]

Current historiography has exaggerated not just the amount of opposition to sports more generally but also the successes that the opponents of sports claimed. Bull baiting and cockfighting were sports already in decline before they came under attack. When we look at their regional distribution, even in the second half the eighteenth century these were already confined largely to relatively small parts of England: cockfighting largely to northern England, and bullbaiting to parts of the midlands. As Griffin's work shows, in most parts of the country bullbaiting simply disappeared with no evidence of any reason, and only in the west Midlands was it contested.[23] They were becoming unfashionable. Sports linked to the elite, such as cricket, hunting or horse racing, continued to thrive, as did some more popular sports. Wrestling matches, for example, were organized by innkeepers in several parts of England and commercialized, semi-professionalized and formalized from quite early on. In 1746, for example, at 'The sign of the Wrestlers' inn at Ipswich, a contest held on a December Monday was advertised between 'the famous Daniel Hargrave' and 'the noted James Burgiss' for a stake of twenty guineas.[24]

Likewise, seeking to identify any clear 'great divide' appears to be futile. The long period from 1660 through to the mid-nineteenth century should be rather seen as a long period of proto-modernity as features of modern sport slowly began to emerge, not in any consistent way, more in some sports rather than others. There were no dramatic moments of transition but rather slow, undramatic series of changes.

The key factors driving such change in the long eighteenth century were already accelerating urbanization and proto-industrialization; the attraction of gambling, not just to the elite, but across society more

---

[22] Tranter, *Sport, Economy and Society.*
[23] Emma Griffin, *England's Revelry: A History of Popular Sports and Pastimes 1660-1830* (Oxford: Oxford University Press, 2005), 223.
[24] *Ipswich Journal,* 17 December 1746.

generally; the existence of a leisure class, largely but not entirely of landowners; commercialization; the advent of newspaper advertising; and better road communications. Each of these was developing with its own trajectory, but they helped drive the transformation of sport as interdependent trends within the macro-transformations taking place in British society from 1660 onwards. These factors came together to begin over time to create a growing demand for sport.

Proto-modern sport: key factors
Economists have identified a phase in the development of modern industrial economies that preceded and created conditions for the development of fully industrialized societies. This was 'proto-industrialization'. [25] Historians of sport now need to explore much more fully that period of proto-modernity in which the conditions for modern sport emerged. Certainly, it is already clear that the threshold for the beginnings of modern sport, at least in some cases and in some regions, can be pushed well before 1800. It perhaps began to emerge over a long period following the hiatus caused by the Civil War and the stress on Puritanism during the Commonwealth. It might even be pushed further back. Taking a cultural rather than a materialist view, the growth of individualism, alongside new forms of community created by the embryonic factory system, and a more general cultural transformation of society, economy and personality appeared concurrently with the scientific revolution and the Enlightenment, finally crystallizing as the industrial revolution spread across England. Early industrial developments in England can be perceived even in 1700 and grew in pace from the 1750s. Even so, as Wray Vamplew points out, the relationship of sport's expansion to industrial developments is less clear than scholars have claimed and needs to be rethought. Stobbart has shown that in many areas the patterns of urban growth appear to have preceded the period of maximum industrial growth by some forty to fifty years and this forces us to rethink the relationship between industrial and urban development. [26]

What are the key factors that influenced the development of modern sport? Some time ago Allen Guttmann argued that modern sport could be viewed as a by-product of the scientific revolution of the European enlightenment. Certainly, some sports picked up on scientific theories. In horse racing, for example, the eighteenth century saw increased

---

[25] For an early study of the literature see L A Clarkson, *Protoindustrialization. The First Phase of Industrialization* (London: Macmillan, 1985).
[26] Jon Stobart, 'An Eighteenth-Century Revolution? Investigating Urban Growth in North-West England, 1664–1801', *Urban History* 23, no. 1 (1996): 26-47.

interest in scientific farriery and thoroughbred breeding records based on heredity.

Modernity is often tied to industrialization, but the industrialization process had a complex chronology, with much variation in its take-up within and between countries and its beginnings found even in the eighteenth century, often in rural rather than urban contexts. As Wray Vamplew (2016) has recently pointed out, 'the role of industrialization is too often taken as a chronological correlation without the causal relationship being fully specified'.[27] The process was long and drawn out, rather than universal, sweeping, and all-pervasive. Initially it was limited, diverse, and regionally confined. However, as Walton has made clear, the protoindustrial characteristics of what would become cotton Lancashire were already discernible in the seventeenth and eighteenth century. Early industrialization provided more reliable income for some workers over rather longer time frames. [28] However this was not widespread until the late nineteenth century.

Adrian Harvey had implied that the beginnings of a commercial sporting culture in Britain appeared in the period 1793 to 1850.[29] He certainly produced much evidence of commercialized sport at that time, but this was not a major shift. More recently there has been an increased emphasis on the commercialisation of sport in the long eighteenth century. Had Harvey explored the earlier period he would have found that the commercialization of leisure was already established in Britain in the eighteenth century and sport played its part.[30] Commercialization has been a feature of sports during many periods, and in many places, across the century, although the proportion of commercialized sports to non-commercialized sport has certainly increased in the past two centuries. However, mass spectator sporting events were much more sporadic in this earlier period.

Equally significant, in my view is that the population of Britain grew rapidly during the early modern period, from around five million

---

[27] Wray Vamplew, 'Sport, Industry and Industrial Sport in Britain Before 1914: Review and Revision', *Sport in Society* 19, no. 3 (2016): 340-55.
[28] J k Walton, 'Protoindustrialization and the First Industrial Revolution in Lancashire' in. *Regions and Industries: A Perspective on the Industrial Revolution in Britain* ed. Pat Hudson (Cambridge: Cambridge University Press, 1989), 42.
[29] Adrian Harvey, *The Beginnings of a Commercial Sporting Culture in Britain 1793-1850* (Aldershot: Ashgate, 2004).
[30] J. H. Plumb, *The Commercialisation of Leisure in Eighteenth Century England* (Reading: Reading University Press, 1973).

people in 1700 to nearly nine million by 1801. Populations were becoming more concentrated in some market and county towns even at the beginning of the eighteenth century. London's growth was rapid and unprecedented, but population growth was also rapid in the counties round London (Middlesex, Surrey, Kent and Essex), the larger regional trading centres and county towns like Newcastle, Liverpool and York, and the flourishing new industrial towns like Manchester or Leeds.[31] Here, as with what have been called the 'residential leisure towns',[32] there was more sustained interest in sports. London labourers' wages were twice as high as they were elsewhere, and through the course of the eighteenth century, real wages grew rapidly for workers in Lancashire, the North East, parts of Staffordshire and West Yorkshire.[33] These towns possessed remarkably young populations. Young people were drawn to urban areas by the lure of regular and full-time employment, and apprenticeship flourished. So, it is unsurprising that these began to provide early forms of more commercialized sport. In the rural south east, rural incomes started to edge up in the early 1700s, giving men more free time for cricket.[34]

Sports attracted crowds and cash. Constellations of demand for sports like horse racing emerged quite early on. There was an increasing concentration of merchant wealth, and a gentry and aristocratic group wealthy though land, agriculture and mineral deposits, with time, spare capital and by no means risk averse.

Other major factors also aided the increased commonality of both commercial and social forms of sport. Firstly, the expansion of provincial newspaper coverage in the first decades of the eighteenth

[31] Peter Clark ed. *The Transformation of English Provincial Towns, 1600–1800* (London: Hutchinson,1984).

[32] Jon Stobart and L Schwarz, 'Leisure, Luxury and Urban Specialization in the Eighteenth Century', *Urban History* 35, 2 (2008): 216-236. Residential leisure towns included Bath, Berwick, Beverley, Birmingham, Boston, Bristol, Bury St Edmunds, Cambridge, Canterbury, Chester, Chichester, Colchester, Coventry, Derby, Doncaster, Dover, Durham, Exeter, Gloucester, Hereford, Hull, Ipswich, Lancaster, Leeds, Leicester, Lewes, Lincoln, Liverpool, Lynn, Manchester, Monmouth, Newark, Newcastle, Northampton, Norwich, Oxford, Peterborough, Plymouth, Portsmouth, Preston, Reading, Rochester, Salisbury, Shrewsbury, Southampton, Stafford, Stamford, Wakefield, Winchester, Windsor, Worcester, Yarmouth, York.

[33] E.W. Hunt and F.W. Botham, 'Wages in Britain During the Industrial Revolution', *Economic History Review* 40 (1987): 380-99.

[34] David Underdown, *Start of Play: Cricket and Culture in 18th-Century England* London: Allen Lane, 2000).

century allowed forthcoming sporting events to be widely publicized. London newspapers were in wide circulation in the first decade of the eighteenth century and by 1708 Worcester, Bristol, Stamford, and Norwich all had provincial presses. Newspaper publicity, and the inclusion of sporting advertising, with its hyperbole and exaggeration, helped transform sporting events like horse racing as well as signifying their politeness to the burgeoning middling groups. They were, as Michael Harris has shown, 'a core element in the construction of an eighteenth-century public sphere', since readers could supply news reports and advertising.[35]

Fig. 2. Lord Bulkeley.

The expansion of the toll road system, from the mid-1700s, coupled with faster and more regular coach transport, produced far more efficient national and regional communications network, allowing spectators and professional sportsmen to travel from further afield. Sports like horse racing, coursing, hunting and cockfighting encouraged the association of like-minded individuals, meeting together at inns and taverns, country houses, hunting lodges and elsewhere. Indeed,

---

[35] Michael Harris, 'Sport in the Newspapers before 1750: Representations of Cricket, Class and Commerce in the London Press', *Media History* 4, 1 (1998): 19-28.

Stephan Szymanski locates English sport's move towards modernity's origin in formal eighteenth-century associativity and sports club creation, not in nineteenth-century industrialization.[36] The *Journal of Sport History* devoted a special forum to the topic in 2008, and more recently Huggins has argued that gambling on sporting events and informal association were initially much more important than formal club formation in sports' spread. [37] In some more vibrant rural parishes sports such as cricket, wrestling or cockfighting could become strong focal points of communal identity. But it was the Georgian gentry's pervading culture of sociability, and the various voluntary elite associations and clubs they formed, which played a more important role in helping to construct an emergent sporting culture. The first formally organized English sports clubs were emerging even in the 1600s, although their membership was often linked to the leisured classes, often aristocrats and the gentry. In archery there were clubs like the Finsbury Archers (founded 1652), the Scorton Archers (1673), or Edinburgh's Royal Company of Archers (1676). [38] In horse racing, Newmarket's Jockey Club was probably founded c 1717.[39] Horse racing provided a convivial focal point for a wide variety of associational cultural forms, highly useful for political interactions, drinking, gambling, and other sporting events such as cock-fighting, pugilism or wrestling. Subscription hunt clubs were beginning to appear by the 1730s and were fashionable by the 1770s though many hunts continued to be run by a single master.[40] By the later eighteenth-century, hunt clubs were even sometimes sponsoring race meetings, especially in the north. An early London cricket club appeared in 1722 and by the 1750s there were growing numbers of formal cricket clubs appearing in London and the south-east, the major ones with some high-ranking aristocratic membership, although teams were made up of players from radically different social backgrounds.[41]

---

[36] Stefan Szymanski, 'A Theory of the Evolution of Modern Sport', *Journal of Sport History* 35, no.1 (2008): 4;

[37] *Journal of Sport History* 35, no. 1 (2008); Mike Huggins, 'Associativity, Gambling and the Rise of Proto-modern British Sport', *Journal of Sport History* (forthcoming).

[38] Linda Troost, 'Archery in the Long Eighteenth Century' in *British Sporting Literature and Culture in the Long Eighteenth Century*, ed. Sharon Harrow (Farnham: Ashgate, 2015), 105-124.

[39] Huggins, *Horse Racing and British Society*, 12.

[40] See *Newcastle Courant*, 17 May 1737. Subscription hunts were becoming fashionable by the 1770s.

[41] Rob Light 'Cricket in the Eighteenth Century', in *The Cambridge Companion to Cricket*, ed. Antony Bateman and Jeffrey Hill (Cambridge, Cambridge University Press, 2015), 26-39.

Some of the features of early modern sport were driven by the existence of a wealthy leisure class of aristocrats, gentry, and others, whose interests were partly urban, through their town houses and London life, but also rural on their estates. Rural sporting developments stimulated inter alia the development of sporting equipment, semi-professional sports people, sporting associativity and rule development. Coursing clubs with formal rules and membership emerged from informal hare coursing in the later eighteenth century. Deer and fox hunting were widely popular. So were shooting and angling, confined by game laws to landlords and estate owners.

Of the factors most vital in driving sport's progress, one was associativity. The other key factor was gambling. Gambling was ubiquitous among all social classes in England in the eighteenth century, and in sport, excitement and economic investment were often inextricably linked. Probability theory emerged during the Enlightenment, with several published works on card games and sport. Indeed in 1792 the early advertisements for the monthly *Sporting Magazine* expected interest from 'the disciples of de Moivre, the votaries of Diana and the frequenters of Newmarket'. De Moivre was a French mathematician whose book on probability theory, *The Doctrine of Chances*, first published in 1718, was prized by gamblers (Diana was the goddess of hunting, and Newmarket the home of the Jockey Club).

For some, driven by needs for cultural capital or hard cash, winning at all costs led to match-fixing. The members of the aristocracy and gentry had the resources and immense appetite for gambling to make high wagers on a regular basis, on a wide range of sports, including horse racing, boxing, cricket and pedestrianism.[42] Those contests involving high stakes attracted interest, crowds and more gambling. By the late eighteenth century even coursing matches between regional clubs were gathering crowds of several hundred people, often with large stakes placed upon the outcome.[43]

Should it be seen as a separate period?
In the case of Britain at least, scholars are now beginning to accept that the early modern period saw the origins of modern sport and in Britain, the nation most rapidly industrializing, it should be characterized as an era of proto-modernity, an 'early modern' period in terms of sport.

---

[42] For gambling on horseracing see Huggins, *Horse Racing and British Society*, 122-152.

[43] Emma Griffin, *Blood Sport. Hunting in Britain since 1066* (London: Yale University Press, 2007), 118.

Indeed, some historians are now trying to argue that it should be seen as a separate and conceptually distinct period. In 2009 Wolfgang Behringer argued that the early modern period was 'not merely as an independent era in the history of sport, but as the formative period of modern sport'. He suggested that the early modern period could be regarded as 'a distinct epoch in the history of sport, since its early days were marked by the advent of important new sports, followed by their decline from the mid-eighteenth century'.[44] He emphasized the high levels of institutionalization and standardization of sports in England. In 2011, Tomlinson and Young followed Behringer in suggesting that modern sports emerged from developments in the early modern era rather than as a by-product of industrialisation. Sport became increasingly institutionalized by the creation and codification of rules, the building of dedicated sport spaces, a European-wide trade in sports equipment, and the emergence of a professional class of athletes, coaches and officials.[45] In 2016, Mallincdrodt and Schattner likewise portrayed it as an 'independent and formative era'.[46]

How convincing is this argument? Clearly, it was a period which had many of the features of modern sport, with rules for sports from horse-racing and boxing to coursing and real tennis being codified, many commercial features of spectacle and performance, and strong links to gambling in many sports. At the same time, however, it is difficult to see the period as a distinct epoch in the history of sport, when there was no distinct break, no clearly defined period. As early as 1991, Dennis Brailsford argued that modern sport was merely an extension of pre-existing sporting practices that changed to suit different social, economic and political circumstances.[47] And there are still major problems with the existing historiography.

How should we move forward?
We still know relatively little about the period. Much is still unknown. Much needs to be re-examined. If we are to push back the current boundaries of our knowledge, we need to widen significantly the range of our source material, move beyond the more prescriptive literature and gain a much better sense of what sport encompassed, what it meant

---

[44] Wolfgang Behringer, 'Arena and Pall Mall: Sport in the Early Modern Period', *German History*, 27, no. 3 (2009): 333, 357.
[45] Alan Tomlinson and Christopher Young, 'Towards a New History of European Sport', *European Review*, 19 (2011): 487-507.
[46] Rebekka Malinckrodt and Angela Schattner, eds *Sports and Physical Exercises in Early Modern Culture* (London: Routledge, 2015).
[47] Brailsford, *British Sport: A Social History*.

to people, and the extent of changes and continuities. There are many sports during the long eighteenth century that have received only cursory attention, from more popular sports such as wrestling or pedestrianism, to elite sports such as hare coursing and fishing. What becomes clear from the limited work done thus far is that the early modern age is much more complex that many writers have indicated. A strong thread of continuity clearly ran through the period. There were groups, often cross-class that showed a strong resistance to change. There were social reformers and religious puritans who were strongly opposed to violence, blood sports, gambling and the drinking associated with many sporting events. While the attitudes, beliefs and actions of the powerful, privileged and rich influenced sporting developments of some sorts, the middling groups and the mass of the population also played a proactive role in many cases.

There are many challenges for those historians willing to explore the proto-modern age, quite apart from the limitations of existing historiography. Major problems concern the sheer breadth, depth and complexity of the sources available to establish a far wider historical context, develop a more grounded chronology and a fuller understanding of the period, and gain a sense of the distinctiveness of and interconnections between different forms of sport. Newspapers increased sporting content only slowly from the early eighteenth century as they began to recognise the commercial potential of such reportage. Horse-racing provided annual calendars of more important meetings from 1728 onwards. The first sport-focused magazine, *The Sporting Magazine*, only began in 1792. This means that other sources assume much more importance to the historian.

Little-read novels, stage plays, published memoirs and other formal written sources become far more central. Surviving family archives tend to originate from gentry and aristocratic families rather than the poor, but contain letters about sporting events, financial records and accounts for breeding, game-keeping and hunting, bills from sporting professionals such as jockeys and trainers, details of sporting wagers, and other accounts. Wills provide much detail about the later life of sportsmen, their wealth and possessions, and their familial and social connections. However, as ever with such material in hand-written form, graphical features and massive variations in spelling create their own demands. Urban records, especially the more detailed ones of county towns like Chester or York likewise contain much relevant material. Georgian paintings and prints, and surviving sporting architecture become key visual sources, despite the challenges of reading contemporary meanings and creating our own interpretations. Court records, such as those of the Old Bailey which offer transcripts of what was said in court, allow us to see how some sports featured in everyday life. Coroners' reports allow the historian an insight into the contexts of some sporting deaths.

The potential is there. Where are the historians to realize it?

2

Muscle Building and Society Bending: The Slow Birth of Irish Bodybuilding

Conor Heffernan

Abstract

In 1946 the British weightlifting and bodybuilding magazine *Health and Strength* included a feature on the inaugural 'Ireland's Best Developed Man' competition, a bodybuilding and physique contest open to Irishmen of varying weight and muscularity. Said by the magazine to be the first bodybuilding contest of its kind in Ireland, the event featured men from across the country attired solely in posing trunks, flexing their trained and oiled muscles for the assembled audience of men, women and children. Using the 1946 contest as a seminal starting point in Irish bodybuilding, the following chapter examines why, unlike other countries, the Irish interest in physique shows occurred so late in the twentieth century. Taking both a transnational and domestic approach, the chapter seeks to understand why, unlike other countries, the Irish interest in physical culture did not manifest itself in physique shows during the period 1900 to 1939.

Keywords: Ireland, Bodybuilding, Physical Culture, Masculinity, Twentieth Century

Introduction

Twelve contestants stood on stage in December 1946 seeking the title of 'Ireland's Best Developed Man'. Gathered in St. Mary's Hall, Belfast, the aspiring bodybuilders and physical culturists ran through their mandatory poses, hoping to impress judge and spectator alike. Done alongside weightlifting and gymnastic competitions, the bodybuilding show was gleefully reported on by *Health and Strength* magazine the following week.[1] Produced in London, but read in Ireland, *Health and Strength* was one of the twentieth century's most popular outlets for British and Irish health enthusiasts. Founded in 1898, the magazine covered everything from yoga to correct diet.[2] Its unnamed reporter,

---

[1] 'Ireland's Best Developed Man', *Health and Strength,* December (1946): 495, 500.
[2] John D. Fair, *Mr. America: The Tragic History of a Bodybuilding Icon* (Austin: University of Texas Press, 2015), 22-23.

relaying the events from Belfast, spoke of glistening bodies flexing and straining on stage. As the men ran through their poses, their numbers were lessened. First to seven and then, in time, to one. Belfast born Mervyn Cotter, a man known for both his weightlifting prowess and impressive physique, was declared Ireland's 'Best Developed Man' in the competition's inaugural year.

Concluding their report, the correspondent claimed that 'so ended the first physique contest to be held in Ireland, and according to results it will not be the last but a forerunner of a series of yearly contests'.[3] This statement, seemingly innocuous at first, was only partially correct. Many competitions were indeed held after the inaugural show and continued almost unbroken, to the current day.[4] This was not, however, the first time that Irishmen had competed in such a manner. Four decades previously, Irishmen had donned posing trunks, taken photographs, and competed in Eugen Sandow's 'Great Competition' of 1901. Done to determine the best developed man in Ireland and Great Britain, Sandow's competition, and Sandow's subsequent magazine competitions, have been seen by several scholars as the first modern physique contests of their kind and a precursor to the sport of bodybuilding.[5] That *Health and Strength*, a magazine founded in 1898, neglected to mention Sandow's shows, or their imitators within the Irish context gives pause for thought.

From 1908 to 1946, no official physique competitions took place in southern Ireland. In Northern Ireland, which was partitioned from southern Ireland as part of Great Britain in 1920, Irishmen continued to compete in magazines and live competitions. At a time when physical culture competitions and bodybuilding shows emerged in Great Britain, Italy, France, Germany and the United States, southern Ireland

---

[3] 'Ireland's Best Developed Man', *Health and Strength*: 500.
[4] See for example, 'Weightlifting Championships in Tralee', *Kerryman*, April 4, 1959, 3; 'Mansion House Muscles', *Irish Press*, June 14, 1969, 8. 'Bodybuilder par Excellence – at 71!', *Kerryman*, August 30, 1974, 12; 'Can Ya Put the Boot In?', *Evening Herald*, September 14, 1984, 27; 'Galway Bodybuilders Savour National Success', *City Tribune*, November 6, 1998, 4; 'TG4's Giant Bodybuilder', *Connacht Tribune*, November 21, 2008, 4; 'Belfast Pumped to Win Bodybuilding Championships', May 29, 2014, 24.
[5] David L. Chapman, *Sandow the Magnificent: Eugen Sandow and the Beginnings of Bodybuilding* (Illinois: University of Illinois Press, 1994), 129; Dimitris Liokaftos, *A Genealogy of Male Bodybuilding: From Classical to Freaky* (London: Taylor & Francis, 2017), 49.

appeared almost entirely disinterested.[6] The reasons behind the south's relative lethargy toward bodybuilding in the opening decade of the twentieth century form the basis of the present chapter. Surveying roughly three decades of Irish history, the chapter argues that southern Ireland's political and economic turmoil, combined with a socially conservative public sphere, delayed the emergence of bodybuilding at a time when the sport's popularity grew elsewhere. Bodybuilding, as a pursuit, is a niche and, at times, subversive pursuit. Its slow growth in southern Ireland nevertheless spoke of much broader societal, economic and political problems plaguing the state.

Fig. 1. Mervyn Cotter, 1952.[1]

The beginning of Irish bodybuilding

In 1898, readers of *Sandow's Magazine of Physical Culture* were met with an exciting and unprecedented announcement. Eugen Sandow, the man many deemed to be the world's most perfectly developed man, was hosting a physical culture competition to determine the best developed man in Great Britain and Ireland.[7] By this point, Sandow had spent roughly a decade in the public limelight, courting worldwide attention from reporters, physicians, politicians and even monarchs.[8] He was, according to his respective biographers, David Chapman and David Waller, the undisputed 'face' of the physical culture movement.[9] Defined by Michael Anton Budd as a late nineteenth and early twentieth century concern with the ideological and commercial cultivation of the body, physical culture, as a pursuit, took hold of the British, and by extension her Empire's, consciousness at this time.[10] Weightlifting and, at times, competitive sport, was labelled as

---

[6] David Webster, *Barbells and Beefcake: An Illustrated History of Bodybuilding* (Irving: Author, 1979), 1-25.

[7] Chapman, *Sandow the Magnificent*, 1-22 deals with Sandow's importance at this time.

[8] Ibid. See also David Waller, *The Perfect Man: The Muscular Life and Times of Eugen Sandow, Victorian Strongman* (London: Victorian Secrets, 2011), 1-30.

[9] Ibid.

[10] Michael Anton Budd, *The Sculpture Machine: Physical Culture and Body Politics in the Age of Empire* (New York: NYU Press, 1997), 152.

physical culture by many as a catch all term during the early 1900s but in the broader British lexicon, the term was applied primarily to the building of the body for the body's own sake.[11]

It is within this context that Sandow's 'Great Competition' must be placed. Announced in late 1898, Sandow's competition was not concerned with finding the greatest muscular bulk but rather with the discovery of a man brimming with vitality. Overall musculature was combined with nebulous ideas like vim and vigour, said to be observable through the health of one's skin, posture, demeanour and so on.[12] Sandow's contest, unlike its later bodybuilding equivalents, was concerned with contestant's overall health. To enter Sandow's competition, competitors were required to take photographs of themselves and submit them alongside coupons available through Sandow's magazine.[13] Photographs were then evaluated by Sandow and his fellow adjudicators in London. The top three contestants from each county were awarded a gold, silver or bronze medal respectively, with the top entrant invited to compete in Sandow's finale at the Royal Albert Hall in London in 1901.

Upon the announcement of the competition, Ed Boyne, a young barber from Dublin, submitted his photograph for consideration.[14] He was followed by countless other Irishmen. Writing in late 1899, Sandow explained that

> In Dublin and Belfast, the competitors if not quite so numerous as in their big English centres, were in an equally forward state of physical development. Schools are about to be opened in the other large cities of the Emerald Isle and if we can take what we saw in Dublin and Belfast as a standard, Ireland will rank with the foremost nations of the world for the physical development of her sons...[15]

By 1901, Sandow's Irish contestants included Roman Catholic Farmers, Church of Ireland Smiths, Church of Ireland Railway Officials and a Protestant Furrier. Class, creed and location varied and differed

---

[11] Thomas E. Murray, 'The Language of Bodybuilding', *American Speech*, 59, no. 3 (1984): 195–206.
[12] 'The Great Competition', *Sandow's Magazine*, 1 (1898): 79.
[13] Ibid.
[14] 'Some Entrants from the Competition', *Sandow's* Magazine, 1, no. 6 (1898): 447; 1901 Census of Ireland, Dublin, North Dock, House 2.1 in Upper Tyrone Street.
[15] 'The Great Competition', *Sandow's Magazine of Physical Culture*, 3.1 (1899): 375-384.

immensely.[16] Owing to a combination of travel logistics, ill luck and, in one case, a very serious illness, no Irishmen attended Sandow's London finale.[17] A precedent had, however, been set. Irishmen had competed in a physique competition. Furthermore, they had done so in a largely respectable way. Margaret Walter's claim that the male nude largely disappeared during the nineteenth century has, in recent years, undergone great historical criticism.[18] Sandow's competition nevertheless had the potential to be seen as lewd and subversive by outside spectators.[19] It was, according to Michael Anton Budd, only through Sandow's keen eye for respectability and promotion that the competition was viewed as acceptable and even, in some quarters, as scientific.[20]

In the wake of Sandow's 'Great Competition', the strongman held several additional physical culture competitions through his magazine. Irishmen thus entered Sandow's 'Empire Competition' and, even, his 'Best Developed Baby' competition, the latter of which was won by six-month-old William Bobs Whitmore from Dublin, in 1906.[21] Important though it was, Sandow's competition was not the only physique-based outlet for Irishmen. In 1908 a 'Physical Development' competition was held in Dublin's Empire Palace Theatre. Advertisements for the 'Amateur Athletic Tournament' began in Irish newspaper in March 1908 with 6 April ultimately chosen as the date for the live event.[22] The event provided an indication that the physique associational cultures found in England, had come to Ireland.

Thus far, it has proven impossible to discover how many men entered the contest. That advertisements produced in the lead up to the event noted 'enormous numbers of entries from all parts' suggests that it was well attended.[23] Many of the contestants took part in several of the

---

[16] Conor Heffernan, 'The Irish Sandow School: Physical Culture Competitions in *fin-de-siècle* Ireland', *Irish Studies Review* (2019): 1-20.

[17] Ibid.

[18] Margaret Walters, *The Nude Male: A New Perspective* (London: Paddington Press, 1978), 228; Anthea Callen, 'Doubles and Desire: Anatomies of Masculinity in the Later Nineteenth Century', *Art History*, 26, no. 5 (2003): 669.

[19] Fae Brauer, 'Virilizing and Valorizing Homoeroticism: Eugen Sandow's Queering of Body Cultures Before and After the Wilde Trials', *Visual Culture in Britain* 18, no. 1 (2017): 35-67.

[20] Budd, *The Sculpture Machine*, 108.

[21] *Sandow's Magazine of Physical Culture, Vol. VIII, January to June (1902)* (London: Harrison & Sons, 1902), 67-68.

[22] 'Amateur Athletic Tournament', *Freeman's Journal*, March 28, 1908, 6; 'Amateur Athletic Tournament', *Evening Herald*, April 6, 1908, 4.

[23] 'Amateur Athletic Tournament', *Evening Herald*, April 6, 1908, 4.

events, including the eventual winner of the physical development contest, W.N. Kerr, who competed in the wrestling contests. Two years previously Kerr told the English physical culture periodical, *Vitality* magazine, that while 'I cannot boast of very large muscles yet', he had begun his interest in physical culture.[24] By 1908, he had bested several others in Ireland's first recognisable bodybuilding show. Kerr's bodybuilding title went unchallenged until 1946 when physique competitions emerged once more for the whole of Ireland. In Northern Ireland from 1918 to 1939 men continued to submit photographs to numerous physique competitions often held on a monthly basis in British bodybuilding periodicals.[25] Southern Irishmen, on the other hand, were almost entirely absent from such shows. Similarly, no physique competitions took place in southern Ireland from the outbreak of the Great War until the late 1930s. The absence of southern Irishmen from such competitions and the 'slow birth' of Irish bodybuilding was predicated on warfare, social conservatism and economic downturns.

A STRIKING EXAMPLE OF MUSCULAR POWER

Fig. 2. W.N. Kerr, c. 1908.[1]

Physical culture and the decade of revolution

Michael Anton Budd and James Campbell have both remarked upon the impact the Great War had on systems of physical culture.[26] For Campbell, the realities of warfare forced changes in military physical culture, whose effects were keenly felt in the following decade.[27] Budd, on the other hand, examined the manner in which the Great War exposed many of the frailties underlying recreational physical culture.[28] Indiscriminate loss of life, material shortages and deprivation were contrasted with older conceptions of Edwardian physical culture. Put

---

[24] W.N. Kerr, 'Letter from Dublin', *Vitality,* 9, no. 1 (1906): 19-20.

[25] See for example, 'Ireland Stepping Forward - League Gala and Carnival Successes', *Health and Strength,* 41, no. 7 (1927): 180; 'Offer to Belfast Paladins', *The Superman,* 4, no. 6 (1933): 290; 'Superman Course Competition', *The Superman,* January (1933): 47.

[26] Budd, *The Sculpture Machine,* 110-114; James D. Campbell, *'The Army Isn't All Work': Physical Culture and the Evolution of the British Army, 1860–1920* (London: Routledge, 2016), 145-192.

[27] Campbell, *'The Army Isn't All Work',* 193-211.

[28] Budd, *The Sculpture Machine,* 110-114.

simply, it was impossible to celebrate the body at a time when soldier mortality was staggeringly high. The War was also said to have materially impacted physical culturists. More than one physical culturist, including the great Eugen Sandow, went bankrupt during the conflict.[29] Several physical culture periodicals were forced to close and those that remained open struggled to meet print runs. *Health and Strength* was one of the few periodicals to remain in operation but its shortened content, oftentimes totalling just four pages, paled in comparison with the previous decade.[30] Printing on cheap pulp paper, the magazine became a jingoistic mouthpiece for the war effort. That no physique competitions were held during this time, in print or in person, was telling of the War's impact in civilian life.

In Ireland, the outbreak of war had two effects. First it negatively impacted recreational outlets for physical culture by restricting the number of physical culture periodicals available in the country.[31] The financial strains imposed by war resulted in the closure of several large-scale gymnasia, many of which remained closed for the remainder of the decade. The Dublin Physical Culture Society, which boasted several hundred members in 1914, was forced to close sometime the following year, only to reopen again in the mid-1920s.[32]

War also affected the main audience for physical culture, namely young men with disposable income. The displacement of men from Ireland was smaller than France or England but its impact was nevertheless important. [33] David Fitzpatrick previously estimated that roughly 200,000 Irishmen enlisted, a figure that represented roughly ten percent of the adult male population in Ireland. [34] This ten percent was, however, primarily composed of men between the ages of eighteen and thirty-five, the prime physical culture demographic.

---

[29] Chapman, *Sandow the Magnificent*, 170, Budd, *The Sculpture Machine*, 110-114.
[30] Ana Carden-Coyne, *Reconstructing the Body: Classicism, Modernism, and the First World War* (Oxford: Oxford University Press, 2009), 169-200.
[31] The impact of war is reiterated in 'Trekking Homewards', *Health and Strength*, 24, no. 17 (1919): 248.
[32] J.M.N., 'Irish Girl Gymnasts', *Weekly Irish Times*, October 27, 1923, 10.
[33] Jay M. Winter, 'Britain's Lost Generation of the First World War', *Population Studies*, 31, no. 3 (1977): 449-466; Leonard V. Smith, *The Embattled Self: French Soldiers' Testimony of the Great War* (New York: Cornell University Press, 2014.
[34] David Fitzpatrick, 'Militarism in Ireland, 1900-1922,' in *A Military History of Ireland*, ed. Thomas Bartlett and Keith Jeffrey (Cambridge: Cambridge University Press, 1996), 388.

Group taken at the fancy dress dance, given by the Dublin Physical Culture Society, on Monday night at Mr. Leggett Byrne's dance hall.

Fig. 3. Dublin Physical Culture Society, c. 1928.[35]

The impact of the Great War on Irish society and politics from 1914 to 1918 has long attracted historical attention. Aside from the impact accruing from the European conflict, the period 1914 to 1918 witnessed seismic domestic changes in Ireland. A nationalist insurrection against British rule took place in Ireland in 1916. Lasting only five days, the '1916 Rising', represented the first in a series of revolts against British rule in Ireland. Following a wave of mass arrests in the wake of the Rising, public sentiment in Ireland became decidedly more nationalist. The period 1917 to 1919 saw nationalists consolidate their support by running for political office, mobilizing supporters and training men for impending conflict. On 21 January 1919, the first shots of the Irish War of Independence rang out. Fought largely between the Irish Republican Army (IRA) and British forces in Ireland, the conflict, lasted for two years, ending in late 1921 when southern Ireland achieved political independence from Great Britain.[36]

Where does physical culture and bodybuilding fit into this history? The move towards nationalist warfare in Ireland, in both 1916 and subsequently 1919, was, in part, fuelled by physical culture practices.

---

[35] 'Group Photo of Dublin Physical Culture Society', *The Irish Times*, January 25, 1928, 9.
[36] Diarmaid Ferriter, *A Nation and Not a Rabble: The Irish Revolution 1913-1923* (London: Abrams, 2017).

Prior to 1916, several of the leading members of the Rising used physical culture, either personally or as a means of strengthening bodies with an eye to political freedom.[37] Patrick Pearse, an Irish cultural nationalist, insisted that the physical culture taught at his school, St. Enda's Rathfarnham, was combined with a nationalist ethos.[38] Pearse's efforts to combine physical culture and nationalism was echoed by *Na Fianna Éireann*, a nationalist equivalent to Lord Baden-Powell's Boy Scouts. Led by later members of the 1916 Rising, recollections from *Na Fianna* stressed the importance of exercise as a political project. This was not a trivial point.[39] During the Irish War of Independence, the IRA actively recruited physical culture instructors to train men in physical drill. This was the case for Thomas Halpin, drilled by 'Old Horse', Joe O'Neill. As a brother-in-law of an IRA officer, O'Neill was co-opted into training IRA recruits before the RIC persuaded him to cease.[40]

The IRA's keen interest in physical culture for political, as opposed to aesthetic, reasons soon paid dividends in battle. Diarmaid Ferriter previously highlighted the nationalist's reputation among British officers for its corps of physically fit and strong troops. Ferriter has also stressed the importance of physical fitness to the war effort, noting the vast distances guerrilla fighters travelled to engage with British combatants.[41] Individual soldiers, like Tom Barry, Geoffrey Ibberson and Maurice Donegan, later spoke of the importance physical culture played in their ability to continue fighting.[42] Physical culture and an interest in the body did not disappear during the 'decade of revolution', in fact it was arguably heightened. What had changed, dramatically, was its emphasis.

From 1914, physical culture in Ireland became increasingly politicised. Whereas pre-war physical culture was, with the exception of the

---

[37] Pádraic Pearse, *To the Boys of Ireland in Political Writings and Speeches* (Dublin: Phoenix, 1924), 114; Honor O'Brolchain, *Joseph Plunkett: 16 Lives* (Dublin: O'Brien, 2012), 46.

[38] Elaine Sisson, *Pearse's Patriots: St Enda's and the Cult of Boyhood* (Cork: Cork University Press, 2004), 115-130.

[39] Marnie Hay, 'An Irish Nationalist Adolescence: Na Fianna Éireann, 1909–1923', in *Adolescence in Modern Irish History*, eds. Susannah Riordan and Catherine Cox (London: Palgrave, 2015), 103-128.

[40] Bureau of Military History Witness Statement 742 (Thomas Halpin, Cork), 24-25. Available at: http://www.bureauofmilitaryhistory.ie. Henceforth BMH WS.

[41] Diarmaid Ferriter, *The Transformation of Ireland, 1900-2000* (London: Gardners Books, 2005), 144.

[42] Tom Barry, *Guerrilla Days in Ireland: A First-hand Account of the Black and Tan War (1919-1921)* (New York: Devin-Adair Company, 1956), pp. 16-20; BMH WS 1307 (Geoffrey Ibberson, Mayo), 3; BMH WS 639 (Maurice Donegan, Cork), 4.

military, largely divorced from political appropriations, the 'decade of revolution' saw a noticeable shift from recreational to politicised exercise. In the lead up to the 1916 Rising, Irishmen, and, to a lesser extent, Irish women, were prepared for battle through the use of physical culture exercises. [43] When the Great War ended in 1918, Irishmen returning home from battle were actively recruited by Irish and British forces to take part in an upcoming conflict. Once more physical culture systems of exercise came to play a role in preparations. [44] Warfare directed men's attentions away from recreational physical culture during an already tumultuous period. In England in 1919, *Health and Strength* and other periodicals began to resume their physique contests as gymnasiums re-opened around the country.[45] Indeed, Anna Cardon-Coyne has found that the return of injured soldiers in 1918 and 1919 precipitated a resurgence of interest in the body.[46] This was not the case in Ireland where the outbreak of the War of Independence (1919-1921) diverted men's attentions away from the recreational physical culture that underpinned bodybuilding competitions.

For those uninterested in revolt, this turn in physical culture was hard to escape. Commenting on the stagnation of Irish physical culture in the mid-1920s, J. Maxwell Neilly, a physical culture writer of the pre-war period, cited the large rate at which gymnasiums closed during the War of Independence.[47] Neilly complained that the destruction wrought by guerrilla warfare, combined with a loss of members, forced innumerable men and women to exercise without a gymnasium or instructor. Further exacerbating matters was a subsequent Civil War in southern Ireland from 1923 to 1924, which intensified these closures. In his pre-war journalism, under the *nom de plumb* of 'Huck Finn', Neilly was one of Ireland's most enthusiastic physical culture proponents. [48] Further evidence can be found in *Health and Strength* magazine. In 1923, in the midst of the Civil War, one unnamed correspondent wrote of Dublin's

---

[43] Ibid.

[44] Paul Taylor, *Heroes or Traitors? Experiences of Southern Irish Soldiers Returning from the Great War 1919-1939* (Liverpool: Liverpool University Press, 2015), 19-74.

[45] See for example 'League Notes & News', *Health and Strength,* 30, no. 17 (1922): 252.

[46] Carden-Coyne, *Reconstructing the Body*, 165-180.

[47] J.M. Neilly, 'Sport in Ireland To-Day: Dublin Gymnasts and the Tailteann', *Health and Strength*, 31, no. 14 (1922): 21.

[48] 'The Late Mr. J. M. Neilly', *The Irish Times*, January 30, 1924, 7.

dangerous environment, which he believed discouraged physical activity.

> To me Dublin, on Saturday night and for days before, was as a city where dire trouble was openly, blatantly courted, guns were terrible in their plenitude...[49]

Three decades later, Leo Bowes, an Irish strongman, dedicated a series of articles in his 'Irish Notes' section in *Health and Strength* on the Civil War's impact on Irish gymnasiums. His readers soon reached out with their own stories, as was the case with J.J. Collier in 1951.

> Old time Dublin physical culturist and cyclist, J.J. Collier is anxious to contact ex members of the now defunct Dublin Colossus PC Club. Flourishing in the days of Sandow, the club was obliged to close its shutters when civil war ravaged the Emerald Isle around 1921-1922...[50]

This situation echoed broader sporting pursuits, like the GAA. As explained by Paul Rouse, the GAA, although still popular, struggled to attract the same attention from Irishmen during this period.[51] Whereas southern Irish physical culture was greatly impacted by conflict and warfare, northern physical culturists were given far more freedom to indulge their interest in bodybuilding. From the mid-1920s images of Northern Irishmen began appearing in the monthly physique competitions held in English periodicals like *Health and Strength* or *Superman*.[52] These magazines, which at times lamented the absence of southern Irishmen, provided a sustained outlet for those in the North to resume their interest in physique competitions.[53] In southern Ireland, the continued conflict diverted men's attentions away from physical culture towards more politicised forms of exercise. Furthermore, it

---

[49] 'A Dublin Nightmare: Why Siki and McTigue Defied Rebels', *Health and Strength*, 32, no. 13 (1923): 99.

[50] Leo Bowes, 'Gossip from the Emerald Isle', *Health and Strength*, 80, no. 19 (1951): 46.

[51] Paul Rouse, 'The Triumph of Play', in *The GAA and Revolution in Ireland 1913-1923*, ed. Gearoid Ó Tuathaigh (Cork: Collinspress, 2015), 33-36

[52] See Thomas McMullar, 'Among the Ulster Gymnasts', *Health and Strength*, 31, no. 23 (1922): 360; 'Ireland Stepping Forward - League Gala and Carnival Successes', *Health and Strength*, 41, no. 7 (1927): 180; 'Offer to Belfast Paladins', *The Superman*, 4, no. 6 (1933), 290; P. Kelly, 'Irish Ideas', *The Superman*, 7, no. 2 (1936), 71.

[53] 'A Dublin Nightmare'.

forced gym closures for those who interest in exercise was already being tested.

Physical culture in a conservative state
Warfare was not the only factor that limited physical culture in the Irish Free State that emerged in southern Ireland post-1923. Just, if not more important, was the socially restrictive atmosphere that accompanied independence. Senia Pašeta previously highlighted the socially and politically conservative world that was the Irish Free State. [54] This conservatism was, in part, a continuation of previous censorship trends found at the beginning of the century. [55] What differed post-independence, was that Ireland's first government, in the guise of Cumann na nGaedhael, took a much more prominent position in the wider society. Traditionally Cumann's conservative nature has been studied with reference to the government's, at times draconian, efforts to make the new nation state economically viable.[56] The government's social conservatism was equally important. Indeed, for physical culturists, the introduction of the Censorship of Publications Act of 1929 had great ramifications for their access to information.

In 1931, and subsequently in 1933 when Fianna Fáil came to power, a series of physical culture magazines were officially censored owing to policies enacted under Cumann na nGaedheal. [57] Critically these included previously accessible and popular periodicals like *Health and Strength* or *Health and Efficiency*. Some, like Bernarr MacFadden's *True Crime* and physical culture periodicals were censured in several states.[58] Unfortunately, the minutes surrounding the decision to ban physical culture magazines in Ireland no longer exist. That the decision was taken at all was nevertheless illustrative of the problems facing southern Irish bodybuilders seeking information about their pursuit.

The late nineteenth and early twentieth century witnessed the emergence of several dozen physical culture periodicals in Ireland from

---

[54] Senia Pašeta, 'Censorship and its Critics in the Irish Free State 1922-1932, *Past & Present*, 181 (2003): 193-218.
[55] Kevin Rafter, 'Evil Literature: Banning the News of the World in Ireland', *Media History*, 19, no. 4 (2013): 408-420.
[56] Jason Knirck, *Afterimage of the Revolution: Cumann na nGaedheal and Irish Politics, 1922–1932* (Wisconsin: University of Wisconsin Pres, 2014), 1-22.
[57] Irish Censorship Board, *Censorship of Publications Acts, 1929 to 1967, Register of Prohibited Publications* (Dublin: Stationery Office, 1946).
[58] William H. Taft, 'Bernarr MacFadden: One of a Kind', *Journalism Quarterly*, 45, no. 4 (1968): 627-633.

England, France and the United States.[59] While the popularity of these periodicals was negatively impacted by the conflict previously examined, their pre-war popularity was undeniable. Men submitted photographs of themselves to *Sandow's Magazine of Physical Culture* on a regular basis, Irish newspapers modelled their own physical culture columns on foreign counterparts while foreign periodicals devoted space for Irish affairs. The content of these magazines did not appear to differ greatly in the 1930s than the 1900s except for one noticeable exception. As detailed by Michael Hau in his work on German physical culture, the interwar period saw nudism emerge as a sustained interest in physical culture periodicals.[60] The same was true for British periodicals, including *Health and Strength*.[61] Articles promoting nudism, and a general comfort with naked bodies, may have influenced the censorship of these periodicals in southern Ireland. It is notable in this regard that the sole Irish contribution on nudism to these magazines during the 1930s was from Bob Tisdall, an Irish Olympian runner who spent the majority of his time outside of Ireland.[62]

Whatever the reasons behind the censorship decisions, the removal of physical culture and bodybuilding periodicals hampered southern Irish bodybuilding interests. In England, a Mr. Britain contest was promoted by *Health and Strength* in 1930 following a series of regional contests during the 1920s.[63] In Europe and the United States a series of bodybuilding competitions were created during this period.[64] These shows, often promoted and sustained by physical culture magazines, offered a platform to compete in physique competitions. At a time when these contests grew in popularity, southern Irishmen were denied even the most rudimentary forms of platforms in the guise of periodicals. Where the decade of conflict resulted in a series of gym closures, the 1930s saw censorship take hold. These restrictions were exacerbated by the economic problems plaguing southern Ireland.

---

[59] Heffernan, 'The Irish Sandow School'.

[60] Michael Hau, *The Cult of Health and Beauty in Germany: A Social History, 1890-1930* (Chicago: University of Chicago Press, 2003), 3-16.

[61] Annebella Pollen, 'Utopian Bodies and Anti-Fashion Futures: The Dress Theories and Practices of English Interwar Nudists', *Utopian Studies*, 28, no. 3 (2018): 451-481.

[62] Neville Buckley, 'Science of Nakedness: Nudist or Sunbather?', *The Superman*, 3, no. 5 (1933): 21-22.

[63] John D. Fair, 'Oscar Heidenstam, The Mr Universe Contest, and the Amateur Ideal in British Bodybuilding', *Twentieth Century British History*, 17, no. 3 (2006): 396–423.

[64] Fair, *Mr. America*, 12-20.

Economic wars and makeshift equipment

Cumann na nGaedhael's tenure in office from 1923 to 1932 was characterised by the party's staunch efforts to avoid excess spending and balancing of the budget. For many, the government's commitment to balancing Ireland's budget was most forcefully demonstrated in 1924 when the old age pension was lowered from ten shillings to nine. Supporting the decision in Ireland's national chamber, one member earnestly claimed that 'some may have to die in this country and die of starvation' lest Ireland lose her financial stability.[65] These measures, although arguably successful in achieving the government's aims, bred ill will among the populace. Matters worsened after 1929 when a global depression set across much of Europe and the United States. Southern Ireland was arguably better equipped to deal with an economic downturn owing to the government's policy, but the economy still suffered.[66]

Despite Cumann na nGaedhael's adherence to budget balancing, the party believed in free trade. In contrast, and preaching a gospel of autarky alongside promises of increased social spending, Fianna Fáil came to power in 1932 as part of a coalition government. Once in power the party methodically undertake its economic programme.[67] The party's policies included the initiation of a tariff war with Great Britain. In a deliberately provocative act, the Fianna Fáil government withheld the repayment of land annuities to Britain.[68] These repayments dated from the late nineteenth century when Irish tenant farmers were given loans to purchase land in Ireland by the British government.

In response to Fianna Fáil's decision, and exacerbated by the Irish government's increasingly belligerent efforts to increase Irish independence, a series of British governments during the 1930s enacted trade restrictions against Irish goods. In response, the Irish government raised tariffs on British goods, including British iron and steel.[69] While much more work needs to be done on the impact of the 'Economic War' on Irish life away from farming and international relations, there is

---

[65] Fred Powell, *The Political Economy of the Irish Welfare State: Church, State and Capital* (Bristol: Policy Press, 2017), 84-86.
[66] 'Extracts from a Memorandum by the Department of External Affairs on the Effects of the Economic Depression on the Irish Free State', Department of Foreign Affairs (National Library of Ireland, No. 574, DFA 7/55).
[67] Ferriter, *The Transformation of Ireland 1900-2000*, 363-370.
[68] Ibid., 358-372.
[69] Ibid.

evidence it effected recreational pastimes.[70] Physical culture equipment, as typified by dumbbells, barbells or chest expanders was made from iron and steel. From the late nineteenth century, most of the physical culture equipment circulating in Ireland came from Britain. [71] The decision to inadvertently increase the cost of bodybuilding equipment proved problematic for Irish weightlifters.

This misfortune manifested itself in a rather obvious way. It restricted the kind of equipment available in southern Ireland. In Northern Ireland, where access to British goods was largely unaffected, reports on weightlifting regularly discussed barbell sets weighing in excess of 200 pounds.[72] Likewise, heavy dumbbells appear to have been common in many Northern gymnasiums. In southern Ireland, newspaper reports discussing popular physical culture were characterized by their commentary on light dumbbells or light barbells.[73] Where Northern newspapers featured a plethora of advertisements for English produced gym sets, the south's newspapers were noticeably silent. A reason for this was undoubtedly the trade war, which resulted in higher prices for British products.

When a dedicated weightlifting club came to southern Ireland in 1935, in 'Hercules gymnasium', members struggled to provide the same kind of equipment and weights as their Northern counterparts. This was made clear by one member, Eddie O'Regan, who joined the club in 1937 and later recalled the club's initial difficulties in securing the requisite equipment.

> I joined the club...and came three nights a week to work out...The premises were primitive...but what it lacked in fittings it made up in enthusiasm, particularly among the few devoted founder-members who had built the whole thing themselves from nothing. They had scraped and scrounged the few bits and pieces

---

[70] Paul Rouse, *Sport and Ireland: A History* (Oxford: Oxford University Press, 2015), 296-300.

[71] Conor Heffernan, 'Strength Peddlers: Eddie O'Callaghan and the Selling of Irish Strength', *Sport in History*, 38, no. 1 (2018): 23-45.

[72] See 'Ireland Stepping Forward – League Gala and Carnival Successes', *Health and Strength*, 41, no. 7 (1927): 180 or 'Advertisement', *Belfast Newsletter*, August 1, 1938, 12.

[73] This was not lost on others. J. Comerford, 'Physical Culture', *Evening Herald*, February 17, 1936, 6.

together practically out of thin air. Considering most of them were unemployed...it was a remarkable achievement...[74]

It would take at least another decade before recognizable gym equipment came to the south at affordable prices.[75] Aside then from the overall decrease in purchasing power among Irish citizens in the 1930s owing to the global downturn and economic war, enthusiastic Irishmen in the south did not appear to have access to the same equipment as their northern or English counterparts. The south's unique social, political and economic history coalesced to inadvertently deprive those with an interest in bodybuilding of the platform, equipment and environment for the sport.

Conclusion
In late 1939, a 'Keep Fit Crusade' from Dublin announced its intention to host a 'Dublin's Perfect Man' competition. Advertised several weeks prior to its finale, the competition, at first glance, appeared to mark a move towards some form of bodybuilding. Reality proved otherwise. Hampered by a string of delays and postponements, the Committee stressed that the contest was not a physique competition but one exploring every aspect of Irish masculinity from personality to occupation. Budding Irish bodybuilders needed to wait another seven years for a recognized contest.[76]

How and why did bodybuilding become possible? There appear to be three answers. First, a series of weightlifting competitions emerged between southern and Northern Irish weightlifting clubs in the mid-1930s.[77] Opportunities to meet and socialise with men from other clubs and regions strengthened cross boarder collaborations. It was for this reason that the contestants for the previously mentioned 1946 contest came exclusively from weightlifting clubs which had competed against one another from 1935.[78] Second and although not officially stated, censorship on British bodybuilding magazines in southern Ireland appears to have lessened prior to the Second World War. Southern Irishmen's submissions to these magazines increased from 1938 and

---

[74] Eddie O'Regan, 'Reminisces' (Hercules Gymnasium, Lurgan Street Dublin, Private Records).
[75] 'Irish Amateur Lifers', Health and Strength, 74, no. 51 (1945): 455.
[76] 'See and Enter for 'Dublin's Perfect Man' Contest', *Evening Herald*, January 26, 1939, 7.
[77] O'Regan, 'Reminisces'.
[78] 'Ireland's Best Developed Man'.

became a regular occurrence in the next several decades.[79] Hercules member, Eddie O'Regan, later recalled the enthusiasm with which *Health and Strength* magazine was passed around the Dublin club in the late 1930s.[80] Aside from providing inspiration, the magazine gave Irishmen a long-denied platform to display the body beautiful. Finally, the intensification of bodybuilding in Britain in the early 1940s, as promoted by *Health and Strength* magazine, appears to have provided some form of incentive for Irish bodybuilders to hold a contest of their own.[81]

For those in Northern Ireland, bodybuilding and physique competitions had been a long established, albeit niche, form of sport. Temporarily dipping in popularity during the Great War, the 1920s and 1930s saw dozens of Northern Irishmen submit photographs to British physical culture journals as part of their regular physique contests. Southern Irishmen, on the other hand, were virtually absent from bodybuilding contests during the 1920s and 1930s. Owing to a series of social, political and economic barriers, bodybuilding, as a sport, was simply not possible. In the past Irish historians have examined the barriers to sport in individual Irish regions.[82] Bodybuilding, as a sport, is admittedly a far more niche than soccer, rugby or the GAA. Its slow growth in Ireland nevertheless spoke once more of the importance of place and space in one's ability to engage in physical activity.

---

[79] See M.F., 'The Question Box', *The Superman*, 9, no. 4 (January 1939): 106; T. Bowen Partingdon, 'Our Plain Talks Advice Section', Health and Strength, 1009, no. 6 (1942): 118 or Bowes, 'Gossip from the Emerald Isle'.
[80] O'Regan, 'Reminisces'.
[81] Fair, 'Oscar Heidenstam, The Mr Universe Contest...'
[82] Liam O'Callaghan, 'Sport and the Irish: New Histories', *Irish Historical Studies*, 41, no. 159 (2017): 128-134.

3

Students at Play: Sport in the Cheshire County Training College, 1908-1918.

Margaret Roberts and Sarah Webb

Abstract
The introduction of the 1902 Education Act saw wholesale changes sweep the English education system, which established teacher training as a form of higher education. Cheshire Education Authority quickly took the opportunity of the government funds available and in 1908 opened the Cheshire County Training College, a mixed-sex institution in Crewe. This chapter explores the sporting experiences of the students using materials from the College archives, historical newspapers and Education Committee minutes. It is apparent that the collective sporting priorities and opportunities of both sexes mirrored that of the gender expectations prevalent in wider society during the period. Generally, the female students found themselves restricted in terms of time, space and resources, when compared to their male counterparts. This was demonstrated not only by an unequal distribution of sporting finances and facilities but also a comparative low visibility with regards to sport reporting in the student magazine.

Keywords: Teacher-training: Women: Sport: Crewe: Great War

Introduction
The first training colleges for teachers were created in the early part of the nineteenth century, aimed at teachers for elementary schools, there were over 30 by 1850 the majority of which were single-sex and associated with a religious denomination. [1] The wholesale changes instigated by 1902 Education Act, not only introduced the concept of education as a public service, but also established teacher training as a form of higher education. [2] The Act swept away the existing school boards and replaced them with 328 Local Education Authorities (LEAs) who were now responsible for the provision and control of all aspects of education delivery locally, thus laying down the foundation of an

---

[1] Keith Evans, *The Development and Structure of the English Education System*, (Kent: Hodder and Stoughton, 1985), 117.
[2] Stanley J. Curtis and Myrtle E. A. Boultwood, *An Introductory History of English Education Since 1800,* (Cambridge: University Tutorial Press, 1970), 375.

education system still recognized today.[3] By 1904, secular municipal training colleges were recognized and within twelve months the availably of government building grants encouraged many LEAs to provide their own county training colleges; indeed by the beginning of The Great War there were twenty-two such institutions, substantially increasing the number of training places available.[4]

Cheshire LEA, buoyed by innovative ideas that Chairman Dr William Hodgson bought back from a trip to America, quickly drew up plans for their own partly residential, mixed-sex training college.[5] However, the wheels of planning are never easy or swift and the need for teachers was pressing, so while a suitable site was acquired and dedicated buildings were approved and constructed, the Education Committee leased rooms at the Mechanics Institute (MI) in the centre of Crewe, appointed staff and enrolled students and on 5 September 1908, the inauguration of the Cheshire County Training College, Crewe (hereafter referred to as CCTCC or the College) took place. The local newspapers noted the event as marking an important epoch in the history of the county from an educational standpoint, further praising Cheshire for its commendable enterprise and genuine enthusiasm, which other counties would undoubtedly follow.[6] The whole ceremony was completed 'amid a flourish of trumpets'.[7]

Life at the Mechanics Institute
The College was housed at the MI for the first four years of its life and it was the 93 men and 146 women,[8] who were trained during those four years, that established the sporting reputation of the College.[9] The

[3] Harold C. Dent, *The Training of Teachers in England and Wales 1800-1975* (London: Hodder and Stoughton, 1977), 59-60.

[4] Derek Gillard, *A History of Education in England*, www.eductionaengland.org.uk/history 2018 (accessed April 15, 2019).

[5] Margaret Roberts and Sarah Webb, 'Women Educating Cheshire in the 20th Century' (lecture, ManMetUni, Crewe Campus, April 3, 2018); Nora Grisenthwaite and Eleanor M. Reader, *The College in the Green Fields: The Story of Crewe College of Education 1908-1974*, (Crewe College of Education Publication, 1974), 3.

[6] 'Cheshire Training College, Temporary Premises Open at Crewe', *Crewe Guardian*, September 16,1908, 4.

[7] Nora Grisenthwaite and Eleanor M. Reader, *The College in the Green Fields: The Story of Crewe College of Education 1908-1974*, (Crewe College of Education Publication, 1974), 2.

[8] CCTCC Student Register [1908-1931], Sport and Leisure History Research Archive, MMU Cheshire.

[9] Robert Delaney, 'Retrospect', *Souvenir of the 21st Anniversary*, (CCTCC Publication, 1929), np.

cramped temporary conditions that characterized this first stage of the history of the College also helped to develop a supportive interaction between staff and students, creating the close-knit collegiate atmosphere so fondly recalled in later retrospectives.[10] The vigorous community spirit displayed by the young men and women in these formative years resulted in the inception of many of the sports teams, that featured in the College throughout its life, even though facilities for the playing of sport during these early years was difficult.[11]

There was no gymnasium at the MI, rather an large 'Specification Room' that was temporarily fitted with one rope and a set of a parallel bars for the men,[12] taught by Instructor Mr Hanley[13] who had earlier taken a special course in Swedish Drill, at the behest of the Board of Education.[14] Drill, marching and country dancing were all the indoor activities that the women had,[15] and when it came to the appointment of their instructress the Sub-Committee resolved 'to make enquires as to whether her services could be utilised in the Borough in other directions'.[16] Miss Lily Dunn was duly selected and began duties on 1 November 1908, which, alongside her role at the College, were to include teaching physical exercises at Crewe County Secondary School as well as 'such classes in Physical Education that the Committee may direct'.[17]

Being temporarily situated in the centre of Crewe meant that playing fields had to be rented on the outskirts of town, as evidenced in the Training College Sub-Committee (TCSC) minutes from 1908, which

---

[10] Henry J. Dickenson, 'The Good Old Days', *Old Students Association: Coming of Age*, 1929, 34-36.

[11] TCSC Minutes, Cheshire Education Committee, April 14, 1913; The documents held within the College archives are sparse for the early years but a copy of a college prospectus from 1913/14 notes that students' clubs were managed entirely by their own committees, with a member of staff as treasurer. The annual subscription was 10/- for women and 15/- for men, which covered football, hockey, tennis, magazines and occasional grants to other recreations, such as dancing as well as payments for transport, where needed, to away matches. This prospectus was a duplication of those used in previous years, with minor alterations to term dates, as noted in the above referenced minutes.

[12] Mrs Greenfield, *Some Aspects of Physical Education at CCTCC*, Private Papers circa 1932; the Specification Room at the MI was noted as being 46 feet by 21 feet in size.

[13] CCTCC Staff Register (1908-1959).

[14] TCSC Minutes, Cheshire Education Committee, July 22, 1908.

[15] Marion Stubbs, 'In the Beginning', *OSA Magazine*, 1972. 29

[16] TCSC Minutes, Cheshire Education Committee, July 22, 1908.

[17] TCSC Minutes, Cheshire Education Committee, October 19, 1908.

note a resolution to rent two playing fields on the 'corner of Sydney Road' at a cost of £5 each from a Mr Richards of Crewe Green, for the use of the male students during their football season. [18] This arrangement was repeated up to and including the winter season of 1911.[19] Permission was also given for the purchase, 'not exceeding £30', of a moveable pavilion to be erected on the playing fields for the use of the men.[20] The female students had no such luxury afforded to them, having to be content with the use of the recreation grounds connected with the nearby Ruskin Secondary School, for the 'practice and playing of hockey, where and when possible'[21] and sometimes a share of the football pitch, when not required by the male students.[22]

The fledgling teams of the early days of the College played matches against secondary schools, local clubs and other colleges, travelling to away matches by train, horse drawn wagonette or bicycle. [23] Unfortunately, there are no records of matches played in the College archives during these early years[24] but a number of reports of various games played can be found in the local press including; football matches in 1909 and 1910 against Old Wittonians and St Johns School Whitchurch, CCTCC drawing 2 all[25] and winning 7-2[26] respectively. In 1908 the 'Ladies of Winnington Park were at home to the Ladies of Crewe Training College', who were late in arriving and as 'it seemed very likely that the light would go before the game could be completed, a couple of minutes of time was deducted from each half'. The home team were reported to have held their own against the visitors and eventually won the game 3-1, which was deemed a very creditable

---

[18] TCSC Minutes, Cheshire Education Committee, September 21, 1908; 'Cheshire Education', *Cheshire Observer* Saturday 19 December 19, 1908, 4.

[19] TCSC Minutes, Cheshire Education Committee, April 19, 1911.

[20] TCSC Minutes, Cheshire Education Committee, October 28, 1908.

[21] TCSC Minutes, Cheshire Education Committee, May 17, 1909.

[22] Marion Stubbs, 'In the Beginning', *OSA Magazine*, 1972. 29.

[23] Nora Grisenthwaite and Eleanor M. Reader, *The College in the Green Fields: The Story of Crewe College of Education 1908-1974*, (Crewe College of Education Publication, 1974), 8.

[24] The College archives contain two named pictures of the CCTCC female hockey first XI from the years 1909 and 1910, so clearly teams were engaging with the game; In addition, the archives contain a letter received in 1985 from a Mr James Hibbert informing the College of the death, at 91, of his mother Mrs Sybil Hibbert, nee Booth. His letter recalled how his mother often spoke, with pride, at being goalkeeper and captain of the College hockey team while she was a student as part of the 1909/11 cohort.

[25] 'Sport', *Northwich Guardian*, December 4, 1909, 5.

[26] 'Football', *Shrewsbury Chronicle*, November 18, 1910, 4.

performance.[27] What must have been one of the last matches played while the students were still housed in the MI was against a visiting side from Manchester Day College, the Crewe team being victorious 2-0.[28] Many other matches and sports were played, as made obvious by the various memoirs of ex-students, who recalled their days at the 'old Coll'. in the 1929 *Coming of Age* issue of the Old Student Association (OSA) magazine.[29]

Life on campus
Meanwhile, construction of permanent college buildings in nearby Crewe Green were well advanced and by June of 1911, Mr Beswick, the County Architect, informed the TCSC that the time had arrived when the levelling and formation of the playing fields needed to be undertaken. The final decision regarding the position and number of pitches and courts had to be made in order that work could commence.[30] The eventual layout, shown in *Figure 1* below, had three and a half acres allocated to the recreation of the male students, a football pitch and cricket ground on land behind the gymnasium and tennis courts and lawns to the side of the main education block. However, this amount of land was not agreed upon without some disquiet, when in February 1908, a row broke out at the monthly meeting of the Cheshire Education Committee. The Higher Education Board proposed the purchase of an additional two acres of land for use of the male students, to add to the previously agreed acreage. At a relatively high cost of £605 per acre Professor Gonner, Chair of the Education Committee, demanded to be informed as to the purpose of the extra land. The Board felt that enough land should be available for the men to play football and rugby simultaneously, they did not 'consider it possible to play on just one ground'. Laughter greeted this statement in the committee room with Professor Gonner, in opposing the motion, stating that he did not know of any public school in the country that provided accommodation for both association and rugby football 'so neither should Cheshire'.[31] However, the extra land was eventually purchased and the hired fields on the corner of Sydney Road dispensed with.[32]

---

[27] 'Winnington Ladies Register Another Win', *Northwich Guardian*, November 13, 1909, 6.
[28] 'Ladies Hockey', *Manchester Courier and Lancaster General Advertiser*, February 1, 1912, 2.
[29] Ernest K. Venables, 'Greetings from Japan', *OSA: Coming of Age*, 1929, 37; Salop, 'Lines to the Men's Common-Room', *OSA: Coming of Age*, 1929, 29.
[30] TCSC Minutes, Cheshire Education Committee, June 26, 1911.
[31] 'Cheshire Education Committee', *Nantwich Guardian*, February 12, 1909, 8.
[32] Anon., *The Jubilee Book 1908-1958*, (CCTCC, Publication, 1958), 7.

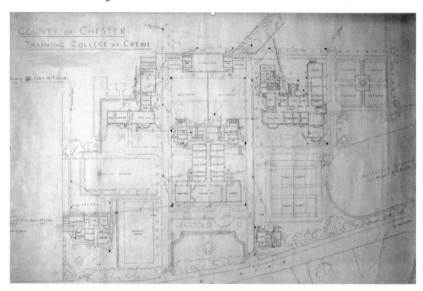

Fig. 1. Architect Plan of the layout of the grounds of Cheshire County Training College, Crewe.[33]

The female students were provided with one and a half acres of land, which was to comprise of a spacious lawn, ornamental flower gardens, a small hockey pitch[34] and tennis courts, all situated close to their hostel.[35] The hopes of the women to have two Fives Courts were dashed early on when the TCSC decided on glasshouses for botanical and horticultural work instead.[36] At one point, the idea was mooted that perhaps the land proposed for the men's cricket pitch at the rear of the College be assigned to the female students as a full size hockey pitch.[37] However, in a sign of the times, Mr Beswick reported that he had interviewed the College Principal, Mr Delaney, in regard to the latter's notion of building a wall, not only between the drill grounds in front of the gymnasium but also between the now two proposed playing fields.

---

[33] Sport and Leisure History Research Archive, MMU Cheshire.

[34] 'News of Old Students', *The Torch*, 1957, 30; Board of Education, Report of Inspection of Cheshire County Training College, Crewe, 1931-32, 17. This inspection noted that the playing field (which was the same space as in 1912), was 'small and does not allow for a full size hockey pitch, being about 20 yards too short and 10 yards to narrow'.

[35] TCSC Minutes, Cheshire Education Committee, June 26, 1911; TCSC Minutes, Cheshire Education Committee, December 11, 1911; The female students were provided with accommodation on campus while the male students were housed in a series private houses in town, selected and approved by the TCSC.

[36] TCSC Minutes, Cheshire Education Committee, October 20, 1910.

[37] 'News of Old Students', *The Torch*, 1957, 30.

The purpose of the wall being to keep the female students respectable and sheltered from the male gaze while in pursuit of their sporting endeavours. Mr Beswick believed such a wall was a superfluous and expensive folly. Mr Delaney, however, partly won the day when it was resolved that a wall between the drill grounds would be constructed but at the expense of the larger hockey pitch.[38]

The exodus across Crewe to the new permanent buildings and associated grounds began in June 1912 [39] with the campus being officially opened on 5 July 1912.[40] The playing fields and gardens were not completely laid out but, under the guidance of the head-gardener, Mr Ravenscroft, student volunteers assisted with the work and soon it became possible to play hockey, cricket, football and tennis within the College boundaries. [41] The new gymnasium, together with the employment of instructress Miss Mary Altham who trained under the methods of the famous Madam Österberg at Dartford Physical Training College,[42] meant that female students now had a more varied indoor exercise regime, [43] including Ling's Swedish gymnastic system [44] as taught at Dartford and although Miss Altham would have come into contact with the relatively new sport of netball, there is no evidence that the sport was played at CCTCC until the 1930s.[45]

Games against old rivals soon recommenced on the improved and enlarged facilities and with the ability to host matches on Wednesdays and Saturdays [46] the College teams could entertain many new opponents, from colleges in Manchester to local clubs and works teams, such as those representing the various workshops at the local railway

---

[38] TCSC Minutes, Cheshire Education Committee, December 11, 1911.

[39] Robert Delaney, 'Retrospect', *Souvenir of the 21st Anniversary*, (CCTCC Publication, 1929), np.

[40] 'Cheshire Training College', *Cheshire Observer*, July 6, 1912, 3; 'Cheshire Training College', *Nantwich Guardian*, July 12, 1912, 3.

[41] Anon., *The Jubilee Book 1908-1958* (CCTCC, Publication, 1958), 7.

[42] CCTCC Staff Register [1908-1959], Sport and Leisure History Research Archive, MMU Cheshire: Miss Altham was appointed in September 1911.

[43] Mrs Greenfield, *Some Aspects of Physical Education at CCTCC*, Private Papers circa 1932

[44] The Ling System was one of several methods of gymnastic instruction.

[45] Netball is not mentioned in the CCTCC archives until the 1931/2 Inspection of the College, where it was noted that the quadrangle used for women students is not large enough to hold a full-sized netball court.

[46] 'Hockey Notes – Season 1914', *CCTCC Magazine*, 1915, 3.

yard. These all contributed to a rapid growth in football, hockey, cricket and tennis on campus.[47]

Fig. 2. Cheshire County Training College, female hostel, with hockey pitch and tennis courts.[48]

The 1912/13 hockey season saw a number of matches arranged for the women of the First XI, who travelled by train to Manchester and together with the Second XI, endured a very cold journey by brake[49] to Northwich, as well as matches against local school teams from Crewe and Nantwich.[50] However, for various reasons, including the problem of a constantly waterlogged pitch,[51] several of the games were cancelled; of the rest, the College team won eight and lost three. The editor of the student magazine noted that the Crewe team were 'decidedly the superior side' in a close 1-0 win against the Old Students of Northwich High School, but that a slow game, 'partly owing to the very small ball' was played against Wincham College, which resulted in the first loss of

---

[47] Robert Delaney, 'Retrospect', *Souvenir of the 21st Anniversary*, (CCTCC Publication, 1929), np.

[48] Sport and Leisure History Research Archive, MMU Cheshire.

[49] A brake was a type of horse drawn carriage

[50] 'Hockey Notes', *The Drift*, March, 1913, 8.

[51] TCSC Minutes, Cheshire Education Committee, February 17, 1913; At this meeting it was resolved to undertake work to drain the excess surface water on the hockey pitch into the nearby Valley Brook.

the season. The Second XI played five matches against Northwich High School, Crewe Secondary School and Chester Ladies; of those it was reported that the game against Chester was the hardest of the season, the visitors being a 'stronger and more practiced team'. The game ended in a 3-0 defeat for Crewe. With the new campus came novel facilities such as dedicated dining and common rooms, which allowed the students to host a post-match tea for visiting teams, followed by singing and dancing.[52]

The male students were able to regularly field both First and Second football XIs during this season, the teams playing twenty-five and seventeen matches respectively, with the match reports in the student magazine being of a more elaborate and descriptive nature than those of the female hockey endeavours. The footballers travelled as far as Manchester to play against the Technical College, the Fallowfield pitch being rated as the best played on, resulting in a fast, open game that saw the Crewe students dominate their opponents, winning 4-1. The November game against the visiting Manchester Training College was the most keenly anticipated match of the season. Unfortunately 'a heavy fall of snow and the intense cold towards the end of the game considerably inconvenienced the players', and the match ended with honours even, followed by an enjoyable evening of 'musical items and dancing'. Games were also played against other Colleges, such as Chester, school teams from Newcastle, Nantwich and Winsford as well as works and church-based teams including Chester YMCA, Nantwich Wednesday, Chester Wednesday, Crewe General Offices, and Northwich Church Lads.[53] The men played rugby but not as often as football, with no reports existing of games in the student magazine and just one newspaper report in 1913, where the College team had 'played a return friendly to the Old Victorians' under the banner of the Northern Rugby League.[54]

During 1913, the swimming enthusiast, second year student Clifford Goss, took on the responsibility of forming a college swimming club and 'induced' several male and female students to form a life-saving class. Students travelled, usually by bicycle, to Nantwich Baths to undergo practice and ultimately two men obtained the Proficiency Certificate of

---

[52] 'Hockey Notes', *The Drift*, March 1913, 8.
[53] 'Football Notes', *The Drift*, March 1913, 10-12; 'Football Notes', *Cheshire Observer*, October 18, 1913, 5; 'Football', *Runcorn Guardian*, September 23, 1913, 6.
[54] 'Northern Rugby League', *Runcorn Guardian*, September 2, 1913, 6.

the Royal Life Saving Society. It was also hoped that an aquatic gala could be held during the Summer.[55]

The 1913/14 academic year saw the cricket team have the most successful in college history, losing only one game from the seven played,[56] with a notable victory against an experienced team of men representing Crewe Railway Station.[57] Along with an improvement of the pitch, situated on the football ground, interest in the game had 'greatly increased' and it was hoped that the present members of the College would carry this keen interest forward to make the following season an even greater success. The good wickets found on the new pitch made home matches an experience 'appreciated by all', thus enabling college cricket to 'have progressed another step'.[58] A heavy roller, at a cost of £7, to help improve the quality of the pitch, had been agreed to by the Sub-Committee before the start of the season proper.[59]

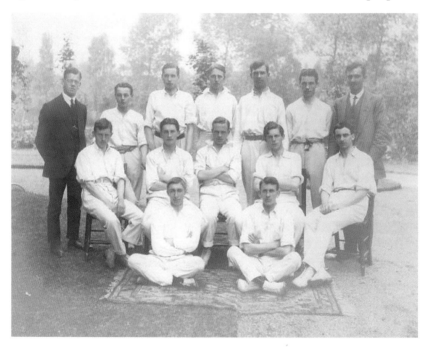

Fig. 3. Cheshire County Training College Cricket XI, 1915. [60]

---

[55] 'Swimming', *CCTCC Magazine*, 1915, 8; The proposed gala was never held.
[56] 'Cricket Notes', *CCTCC Magazine*, 1915, 2.
[57] 'Cricket', *Chester Chronicle*, June 14, 1914, 3.
[58] 'Cricket Notes', *CCTCC Magazine*, 1915, 2.
[59] TCSC Minutes, Cheshire Education Committee, April 20, 1914.
[60] Sport and Leisure History Research Archive, MMU Cheshire.

The female students enjoyed a good tennis season, their early practice games made a lot easier once the funds had been agreed for netting to be erected around the perimeter of the courts.[61] However, when later in the spring of 1914 the surface of the courts began to deteriorate, the request for resurfacing was deferred by the TCSC, although the students were placated with an order for the 'required nets and poles' being agreed.[62]

During the early months of 1914, the swimming club, 'with no man, who is conspicuously enthusiastic', was in danger of folding. It was decided that it was too much to expect 'one man alone' to carry out club affairs, and so a committee, exclusively made up of men was formed. Land-drill classes were undertaken in the college gymnasium,[63] with many of the men reported as performing these exercises exceedingly well. Arrangements were made with Nantwich Swimming Club for the members of the College to join the Club and, it was hoped that during the 'swimming term' large numbers of men and women would 'wheel their way to Nantwich'.[64]

The War years
As 1914 progressed, the students became increasingly aware of the 'overhanging cloud whose gloom makes itself felt on ourselves and everything around us'.[65] The effects of the War on college sport soon became apparent and subsequently reflected in the retrospectives on both the hockey and football seasons. The men, who eagerly awaited their September kick-off, found that the number of matches was considerably reduced, games being cancelled owing to many opposition players enlisting.[66] Similarly, the secretary of the female hockey team commented,

> Living in such troublous (sic) times as these, we can hardly expect to have a perfect season. There was the greatest difficulty in getting matches. Fixtures, for almost all Saturdays and Wednesdays in the season, were arranged months ago, but to our dismay, our opponents wrote one by one to cancel fixtures. But

---

[61] TCSC Minutes, Cheshire Education Committee, April 14, 1913.
[62] TCSC Minutes, Cheshire Education Committee, May 18, 1914.
[63] Land drill exercises, in which students practiced swimming strokes on dry land, were carried out in the gymnasium at College.
[64] Aqua, 'Swimming', *CCTCC Magazine*, 1915, 8-9. The journey from CCTCC to Nantwich Baths would have been approximately 5 miles by bicycle in 1913.
[65] 'Editorial' *CCTCC Magazine*, 1915, 1; The editor Harold Redlar, fell at the Somme, his body never being recovered in the aftermath of the battle.
[66] 'Football Notes', *CCTCC Magazine*, 1915, 4.

in spite of the lack of matches, we have enjoyed our hockey. Practices are almost, if not quite, as enjoyable as matches, and they are made most interesting by arranging such games as Seniors v. Juniors, Blondes v. Brunettes, The aged females v. the infants.[67]

Under the circumstances of the times, the Principal's recommendation in respect of the male students to carry out provisional Military Drill as part of the curriculum was approved by the Sub-Committee,[68] and in this connection Mr Coulson, the Physical Exercise instructor, undertook a Certificate of Efficiency as an instructor of *'Physical Training and Drill: HM Army'.* [69] A notable achievement for the men's football team occurred when student Sydney Pitt was given a trial for Crewe Alexandra in their Good Friday match against Everton. The collegian was reported as doing 'remarkably well in the forward ranks and it was due to his efforts that the Alexandra won by a single goal'.[70]

As the war developed, male students under military age [71] were encouraged to finish their course before enlisting; later, they left as soon as they were of military age. The first student to request to suspend his students was George Gleave, a member of the cricket and football teams, who enlisted in the Army Air Corp in October 1915.[72] In November 1915, the Principal's monthly report submitted to the TCSC, stated that eleven male students had left the College to join the Armed Forces and the Committee resolved that those men who left at half-term be charged half a terms fee.[73] Gradually, as the demands of the services increased, more men enlisted until 'before long the college was practically one for women only, except for a few men, rejects from the services'.[74] In fact, over the course of the War the number of men enrolling in the College

---

[67] 'Hockey Notes', *CCTCC Magazine,* 1915, 3.

[68] TCSC Minutes, Cheshire Education Committee, January 15, 1915.

[69] TCSC Minutes, Cheshire Education Committee, January 15, 1915.

[70] 'Crewe Alexandra' *Nantwich Guardian,* April 9, 1915. 2; Sydney Pitt played for Crewe Alexandra for another few games before he left CCTCC at the end of his course.

[71] During the First World War, the legal age limit to sign up for military service was *18,* and for armed service overseas it was *19.* See https://www.longlongtrail.co.uk/soldiers/a-soldiers-life-1914-1918/enlisting-into-the-army/

[72] As noted in the Student Register [1908-1931].

[73] TCSC Minutes, Cheshire Education Committee, November 26, 1915. The minutes further state that the one student who had left before half-term, namely George Gleave, was not to be charged any fee.

[74] Frederick F.Potter, *Educational Journey: Memories of Fifty Years in Public Education,* (London: Pitman, 1949). 79.

declined so drastically (see Table 1), that by as early as 1916 male team sports became impracticable.[75]

At the December meeting of the Sub-Committee, letters were read from several male staff members, including Mr Coulson, stating their intention to attest for service in the Army Reserve Corp. The opinion of the Committee was that these men were indispensable for the carrying on of the educational work of the Training College and this was to be conveyed to the local Tribunal, with an application to be made for their exemption from Military Service.[76]

Year	Male Students	Female Students
1912	27	36
1913	22	34
1914	21	37
1915	8	37
1916	5	41
1917	5	49
1918	9	40
1919	40 [includes 15 demobilised ex-students]	34
1920	18	40

Table 1. Number of male and female students enrolled at CCTCC [1912-1920].[77]

The steadily increasing number of women students enrolling at the College supported the growing regiments of male students serving in the forces. This was achieved by developing a kind of college home front on campus and they soon found many of their sporting endeavours replaced by knitting parties and the preparation and despatching of parcels to every serving man student whose unit could be traced.[78]

---

[75] As evidenced by the lack of any male team sports reports in the Student Magazines from late 1915 onwards.

[76] TCSC Minutes, Cheshire Education Committee, December 18, 1915; the other members of staff were Mr HV Davies, Science Master and Mr FF Potter, Mathematics Lecturer.

[77] CCTCC Student Register [1908-1931], Sport and Leisure History Research Archive, MMU Cheshire.

[78] 'News of Former Students', *The Torch*, 1965, 51: Robert Delaney, 'Retrospect', *Souvenir of the 21st Anniversary*, (CCTCC Publication, 1929), np.

Carried out under the auspices of the Red Cross and supervised by Mrs Delaney, the principal's wife, the female students helped in every way possible.[79] In addition to studying and teaching practice, all available students worked with Mrs Delaney for much of their recreation time; a party travelled to Dorset to spend a summer holiday flax-pulling, others went fruit-picking or undertook clerical work for the Food Control Board.[80] These activities were just several of the ways in which the women students of the College 'strove to help the nation its crisis'.[81]

Fig. 4. Cheshire County Training College Hockey Team, 1914-15.[82]

The editor of the 1916 student magazine reported that the women's hockey teams had had a successful season, the record of which was posted in the Sports section, which 'is of necessity very small in this number as there has been no football whatever this term. Everybody is now awaiting with eagerness the coming of the tennis season'.[83] The actual report included detailed match results, showing that the First XI

---

[79] The Red Cross card for Mrs Delaney in respect of the students at the College, which notes that amount of time spent on knitting was 'whole', meaning as much time as possible.

[80] Anon., *The Jubilee Book 1908-1958* (CCTCC, Publication, 1958), 8.

[81] Frederick F. Potter, *Educational Journey: Memories of Fifty Years in Public Education,* (London: Pitman, 1949). 79.

[82] Sport and Leisure History Research Archive, MMU Cheshire.

[83] 'Editorial', *CCTCC Magazine*, March 1916, 2.

had won all their matches bar one, a draw against the smaller opponents of Crewe Secondary School, and ended by noting that the Second Xl were 'not so successful as the first team'.[84] Unfortunately, a copy of the magazine for later that term no longer exists and with local newspapers not reporting on any tennis matches, a retrospective of the eagerly awaited season cannot be commented upon.

By mid-1917, with the men being 'very few in number, much of the tradition of the College and many of its institutions relied upon the women for support'.[85] On the sporting field the hockey team were described as having a singularly successful season, with both the First and Second teams not losing a match.[86] Some very hard games were played, with many trips to away fixtures being arduously long, a particular journey to Wincham Hall College, Northwich, taking almost three hours by train and road, including a change at Lostock Graham station, although the students were very pleased to 'all be able to sit in the same carriage' for the whole journey.[87] A few weeks later a match arranged against the Old Students was cancelled as due to the 'great advancement in railway fares eleven old students could not be prevailed upon to pay us a visit'. As in the previous season, many practice matches were undertaken, including, 'day girls against hostel girls', the losers to provide themselves and their antagonists with cake. The women were congratulated for the great enthusiasm shown towards the end of term when the attractions of tennis and the trials of teaching practice provided other interests.[88] The tennis team were almost as successful, losing just one match of the six played. The matches were a contest of nine separate singles games with no double's games reported on. The competition came from Crewe Secondary School, the Old Girls' and local clubs, such as Haslington, Alsager and Weston Lane.[89]

There was always much made of the news of male students serving abroad, with female students spending a lot of their recreation time tracing and writing to serving ex-students and encouraging them to share their news with the readers of the student magazine. The editor of the magazine later reported that 'the general tone of the letters which

84 'Hockey', *CCTCC Magazine*, 1916, 13.
85 'Editorial', *CCTCC Magazine*, July 1917, 2.
86 'Easter Term, Hockey Notes' *CCTCC Magazine*, 1917, 10-12.
87 The same journey today would take half the time by rail and only 30 minutes by car.
88 'Easter Term, Hockey Notes' *CCTCC Magazine*, 1917, 10-12.
89 'Tennis', *CCTCC Magazine*, 1917, 12-13.

have been received is typical – cheerful almost to the verge of recklessness'.[90]

Although the pressure on women was less demanding, there was an expectation that they too should support the War Effort in whatever ways were most suitable, and at the beginning of 1918, the students were saddened to hear that Miss Altham, [91] had her 'sanction' for leave from college, to commence duties with the Women's Army Auxiliary Corps [WAAC], approved by the Sub-committee.[92] To the considerable chagrin of the Principal, she had still not been replaced by the end of the year.[93]

Despite the lack of a qualified instructress, the female students continued with their hockey season, maintaining the standards established by Miss Altham, winning all six matches played. In December, the match played against a team of Old Students was chiefly composed of Seniors, but, once again, travel difficulties prevailed and the single match arranged for the Second XI was cancelled owing to the unsatisfactory state of the away team's grounds. The report finished with a message to the Juniors exalting them to be 'even more successful next season, than we have been this'.[94]

With the return of the men students from the Armed Forces the College started to regain its normal appearance.[95] However, there was a certain hiatus before a full-scale revival of male sport was observed, particularly as some of the men who died on the battle field playing 'the game with straight backs', were the same men who had distinguished themselves and the College on the football and cricket field.[96] By the end of 1918 the student magazine proudly proclaimed that, from the sixteen men on campus a team had been formed that 'once more gained for College a high reputation in the football World. Up to the time of writing we hold an unbeaten record and our hopes are high of maintaining that record'. The first proper match since the end of hostilities was played at

---

[90] 'OSA Column, 1913-15,' *CCTCC Magazine*, July 1917, 14.

[91] Miss Altham returned to CCTCC in 1920, resigning in 1923 to take up the post of Cheshire County Inspector of Schools for Physical Training.

[92] 'Cheshire Training College', *Nantwich Guardian* - Friday 11 January 1918, 6; TCSC Minutes, Cheshire Education Committee, January 5, 1918.

[93] TCSC Minutes, Cheshire Education Committee, December 14, 1918; The Principal informing the committee that the appointment of an instructress for women was now a matter of extreme urgency.

[94] 'Hockey Notes'. *CCTCC Magazine*, April 1919, 11.

[95] 'Editorial', *CCTCC Magazine*, April 1919, 2.

[96] *CCTCC Magazine*, Mid-Summer, 1919, 6.

home against Crewe Secondary School and the men were anxious as to how the team was going to 'shape up' but the result was a slightly disappointing draw. The return fixture a few weeks later, saw the College 'wiping out the disgrace of not winning the first match', with a 6-2 victory. In a sad reminder of the times, the match against Sandbach Grammar School was cancelled due to an outbreak of influenza at the school.[97] The secretary ended his review by thanking Miss Gillett, head of the domestic staff in the male dining room, for ably providing refreshments, often at very short notice. [98] As before the War, descriptions of the football matches were detailed, filling over two pages compared to the single column afforded the women's hockey notes.

The tennis season, although not as successful as could have been wished, was nonetheless, very enjoyable. The team consisted of six senior women students, with juniors helping to referee matches. Only a few competitions were held against outside opponents, those being Alsager Tennis Club and Crewe Secondary School, both resulting in a loss for the College. Other matches involved contests between seniors and juniors, as well as an Old Students team and finally a series of male student against female student encounters. [99] These sporting events were typical of the engagement of students between 1908 and 1918, activities which continued and indeed flourished into the interwar period and beyond.

Discussion
The sporting traditions of CCTCC were established from the very early days, when, despite being under constrained circumstances in the MI, students were keen to participate in the sporting arena. The athletic endeavours of these early students resulted in the formation of many clubs and sports teams, which in turn stimulated much interest in football, cricket, hockey and tennis. The disparity in which the sport of each sex was viewed and played was, however, also evident from the beginning, with playing fields readily hired for the male players

---

[97] The Spanish flu epidemic of 1918-1920, was one of the greatest medical disasters of the 20th century. A global pandemic of an airborne virus which affected every continent. It has been estimated that over 50 million people died world-wide and a quarter of the British population were affected. The death toll was 228,000 in Britain alone. The global mortality rate is not known but estimated to have been between 10% to 20% of those who were infected. See www.historic-uk.com/HistoryUK/HistoryofBritain/The-Spanish-Flu-pandemic-of-1918/

[98] 'Football Notes' CCTCC Magazine, April 1919, 11-12.

[99] Doris Maddocks, 'Tennis Notes', *CCTCC Magazine*, Mid-Summer 1919, 16.

whereas the female students were required to share recreation grounds with local schools or wait until their male counterparts had completed their football games before being permitted to use the pitch.

This state of affairs was to continue even after the College had moved to its own specifically constructed campus. The segregation between sexes, prevalent in society at that time, was manifested not only in the extent of the grounds that was afforded to each gender but also in the use of those areas. The male students were allocated three and a half acres for football, rugby, cricket and tennis, while the women had one and a half acres of land, on which there was a small hockey pitch and tennis courts, with the remainder of the ground being laid to ornamental gardens and lawns.

Further inequalities can be detected in the attitudes of the TCSC when dealing with requests from the College for sporting equipment or maintenance, with no hesitation in awarding funds for instance, to buy a roller for the ground staff to keep the cricket pitch in order but the female students had to wait almost a year for their tennis courts to be surrounded by netting. Even the student magazine allowed more than three times as many column inches when reporting male athletic endeavours compared to those of the females.

With the War raging, the College rapidly emptied of its leading and most enthusiastic athletes and consequently male sport diminished to a point of complete cessation by late 1916. As a result, the women students found that recognition of their own sporting endeavours slowly shifted from the periphery to the centre of the field, in a reflection of the broader opportunities afforded to their sex because of the War.

It should be noted that the women students at the College tended to participate in what were regarded as acceptable female sports, such as tennis, hockey and swimming, as well as activities like gymnastics and country dancing. Football, although increasingly played by young working-class women towards the end of World War One, would not have been considered appropriate for college students aiming for middle-class occupations like teaching and, therefore, the women of CCTCC would not have entertained the prospect of donning football boots.

Conclusion
This chapter explored the sporting experiences of the students at CCTCC during the decade that encompassed the final years of La Belle Époque. Material from the College archives, historical newspapers and Education Committee minutes were interrogated to highlight the

collective sporting priorities and opportunities available to both male and female students, although it should be noted at this stage that the archives are incomplete. From the documents that do survive, it is apparent that the experiences of the women in CCTCC, with respect to participation in sport, mirrored that of gender expectations in wider society during the period in question. Generally, women found themselves restricted in terms of time, space and resources, when compared to men, and for female students at the College this was not only demonstrated by the unequal distribution of sporting finances and facilities but also in a comparative low visibility with regards to sport reporting in the student magazine. Nonetheless, the women played with a zeal and enthusiasm, which they maintained throughout the War years, displaying a collegiality that was also a characteristic of their male counterparts. Future work will include a deeper biographical analysis of this cohort of students, to uncover their individual war experiences and career trajectories as well as any long-term involvement in physical education and sport.

4

The Wheeling Wonders of London: The Lady Cyclists of the Royal Aquarium's First Professional Women's Cycling Tournament

Mike Fishpool

Abstract

The cycling boom of the late nineteenth century saw cycle racing grow as a professional sport, involving both genders. Young women raced on safety bicycles around a wooden oval track in entertainment venues and velodromes, exerting themselves beyond what some parts of society may have considered to be appropriate for the fairer sex. Women's cycle racing briefly captured the public's imagination enabling all social classes to spectate at the races or read about it in popular newspapers. This chapter recalls London's first professional women's cycle racing tournament held in late 1895 at the popular Royal Aquarium and Winter and Summer Garden located in Westminster, one of many races that were held at the venue until 1901. It recounts the racing, the press coverage, and then delivers a biographical history of some of the English riders.

Keywords: Sport, Entertainment, Gender, Women's Cycling, Cycle Racing.

The Six-Day Race, November 1895

Since opening in Tothill Street, Westminster in January 1876, the Royal Aquarium and Summer and Winter Garden had become a major London venue of entertainment, lectures and exhibitions. In late 1895, it held a novel sporting and entertainment event, becoming the first major London venue to hold women's professional cycle races. The competition built on women's races that took place in the summer of 1895 in Hull, Scarborough, Greenock and Edinburgh as part of a British cycling tour, as well as in Plumstead, London. It was the Royal Aquarium's most financially successful event, earning it £4,695 during the first week.[1] Billed as a 'twelve-day race' and taking place in November-December 1895, it featured two separate six-day races each covering one week – except for Sunday to respect the Christian Sabbath.

---

[1] *The Graphic*, January 17, 1903, 15.

A soup-bowl wooden track was laid in the Royal Aquarium's main hall, measuring ten laps to the mile or a total of 11,300 feet (3,453 metres).[2] *Lloyd's Weekly Newspaper* detailed the track, stating that it 'ran round the ground floor, and was formed of pine planking firmly fastened to joists of the same wood, and fenced in by railings. At the east and west ends, where curved round, the outer edge was raised six feet above the inner, to prevent riders flying off at a tangent when negotiating the arc'.[3]

Fig. 1. The Royal Aquarium.

The first six-day race started on Monday 18 November and finished on Saturday 23 November with 20 women entering, comprising 12 French and eight English riders.[4] Organizers were sent to Paris to recruit riders, who were provided with free travel to England, discounts on first class

---

[2] 'The Six Days' International Ladies' Bicycle Race at the Royal Aquarium', *The Sporting Life*, November 18, 1895, 1

[3] 'Lady Cyclists at the Aquarium', *Lloyd's Weekly Newspaper*, November 24, 1895, 11.

[4] 'The Six Days' International Ladies' Bicycle Race at the Royal Aquarium', *Sporting Life*, November 18, 1895, 1; Mike Fishpool, 'Miles and Laps: Women's Cycle Racing in Great Britain at the Turn of the 19th Century – Part II', *Playing Pasts*, September 17, 2018, http://www.playingpasts.co.uk

rail travel and free hotel accommodation.[5] Adverts may have also been placed for the racers – there was at least one advertisement published in *The Era* in September 1895 that pointed to the location and potential time required to race on the track each day, stating: 'Wanted, Ten Lady Cyclists, thoroughly competent to ride in and about London for five hours a day. Fair Ladies preferred'.[6]

The women riders were paid £3 to £10 a week for racing. *The Pall Mall Gazette* reported that this was topped up through prize money and prizes supplied by the Royal Aquarium and individual companies. There was also money paid by bicycle manufacturers and the newspaper identified a wealthy unnamed male benefactor who presented money to riders he liked, providing an example where it says: 'One who was present at this idyllic scene suggested that 'Miss Hutton had ridden very well'. The man of the cheques agreed to this, and, adding that he "must do something for her", handed over a cheque for £50'.[7] The *South Wales Echo* added that the man also awarded the first four positioned in the race £10 each, while the winner received £25.[8]

The riders were dressed in coloured clothing to enable the spectators to identify them. *Berrow's Worcester Journal* described their appearance: 'The costume [...] was a matter which excited much comments. They all wore knickerbockers [...]. The French ladies wore a tightfitting jersey which formed one piece with the breeches and several wore sashes of distinguishing colours. The English ladies wore pretty blouses decked with ribbons, and their hair daintily dressed, while the French ladies wore their hair in plain 'bobs' at the back'.[9] The *Manchester Guardian* added that the 'French girls nearly all wore golf jerseys, full bloomers to the knee, and belts or silk sashes. The English girls had a variety of costumes, about the ugliest being a tight-fitting tailor bodice, worn with knickerbockers, and a skirt drawn up with cords into a tunic. A competitor aged fourteen was got up in tight satin breeches, embroidered stockings, and an elaborate blouse with a scarf'.[10]

The opening day saw the women split into two sections riding a total of five and a half hours. The first section of ten women raced from 14:20

[5] 'How Ladies Races are Managed: A Chat with Mr Ritchie of the Aquarium', *The Hub: An Illustrated Weekly for Wheelmen and Wheelwomen*, September 12, 1896, 221.

[6] *The Era*, September 21, 1895, 23.

[7] 'Whirling on the Wheel', *The Pall Mall Gazette*, November 29, 1895, 11.

[8] 'Present for the Lady Cyclists', *South Wales Echo*, December 3, 1895, 3.

[9] *Berrow's Worcester Journal*, November 23, 1895, 5.

[10] 'Cycling Notes', *The Manchester Guardian*, December 2, 1895, 6.

pm in the afternoon, followed by a second section at 16:45 pm, which contained some of the race favourites. Each section returned to the track again for 90 minutes in the evening.[11] Two representatives from the newspaper *Sporting Life*, which organized the race, were appointed referee and timekeeper. It was started by Edward Du Plat, the Royal Aquarium's exhibition organizer under the direction of the managing director, Josiah Ritchie.[12] The first day was eventful for the spectators with numerous crashes and foul play – the English riders complained to referee Robert Watson about their French rivals, alleging that they were blocking them from overtaking on the outer side of the track with the rules preventing overtakes on the inner side. *The Evening News* reported that 'this unfairness was so marked that it evoked hisses from the spectators'.[13] A band played during the racing, while spectators could also enjoy the Royal Aquarium's other various entertainments and novelties, including dancing elephants, boxing kangaroos, ballet, acrobats, magicians, dancers and comedians. Admission started at one shilling but eventually rose to half a crown and more by the final night.[14]

The racing continued during the rest of the week, culminating in the last day with two races in the evening lasting 90 minutes. The final race featured the French riders Lisette Marton, Marcelle Vautro and Gabrielle Etéogella, and the English riders Monica Harwood, Mrs Grace, Rosina Lane and Nellie Hutton. It evolved into a battle between Harwood and the French champion Lisette. Mrs Grace took up the role of pacemaker as Harwood wearing 'a Union Jack sash' was hotly pursued by Lisette. *Sporting Life* described the end of the race: 'At last the whistle blew, and amidst shouts, cheers, and waving of hats, the end came to one of the most sensational races on record'.[15] It was a victory for Monica Harwood who rode a total of 371 miles and two laps during the entire six days compared to Lisette's 368 miles and six laps. Mlle Cannoe (or Cannac) finished third – she was to be victorious overall in the next six-day race on 2-7 December.[16]

For her win, Harwood was awarded prize money of £100, a purse of gold, a gold and pearl diamond watch, and a gold diamond bracelet.

---

[11] 'Ladies Bicycle Races', *The Standard*, November 19, 1895, 6.

[12] 'The Ladies' Race at the Royal Westminster Aquarium', *Sporting Life*, November 25, 1895, 1. 'How Ladies Races are Managed: A Chat with Mr Ritchie of the Aquarium', *The Hub*, September 12, 1896, 221; *The Pall Mall Gazette*, March 16, 1895, 7.

[13] *The Evening News*, November 19, 1895, 3.

[14] *The Standard*, November 25, 1895, 1; *Sporting Life*, November 25, 1895, 1.

[15] *Sporting Life*, November 25, 1895, 1.

[16] *Sporting Life*, December 9, 1895, 1.

Other prizes for the racers included champagne, fountain pens, clothing and bicycles.[17] There was just over 22 hours of racing during the week. The newspaper *Fun* stated that 'The 'lady cyclists at the Aquarium' entertainment is not so dreary as it sounds. One felt quite a glow of national pride when, at the end of the first week's racing, Miss Harwood (England) was returned victorious over her French rivals. Then the band played 'Rule Britannia'. She rode splendidly and answered gamely to the many shouts of 'Arwood! Arwood!' that sprang from countless throats'.[18]

	Name	Mon 18		Tue 19		Wed 20		Thurs 21		Fri 22		Sat 23		Total	
		M	L	M	L	M	L	M	L	M	L	M	L	M	L
1.	Harwood	56	9	67	3	66	0	59	0	60	2	61	8	371	2
2.	Lisette	56	6	64	9	65	8	59	0	60	4	61	9	368	6
3.	Cannoe	52	5	60	3	63	1	59	0	59	8	61	1	355	8
4.	M. Vautro	52	7	64	8	60	9	58	0	57	9	58	1	352	4
5.	Etéogella	56	8	54	6	60	9	58	4	58	4	59	3	348	4
6.	Lane	49	3	65	1	60	8	55	6	54	6	57	7	343	1
7.	Gamble	51	9	64	3	62	2	54	9	54	7	55	1	343	1
8.	Blackburn	51	0	64	8	60	8	44	3	56	8	56	8	334	5
9.	Grace	14	7	67	0	66	2	58	4	60	1	61	0	327	4
10.	Hutton	30	5	61	5	60	5	57	6	57	7	57	5	325	3
11.	Reillo	52	8	43	4	60	3	53	9	58	2	53	8	322	4
12.	Solange	52	7	45	1	63	0	39	0	39	6	56	4	295	8
13.	Lutreille	39	7	61	5	54	3	48	1	50	3	36	2	290	1
14.	F. Vautro	22	9	49	6	57	9	48	3	49	9	25	9	254	5
15.	Paillarde	-	-	68	5	61	0	47	1	52	1	18	4	247	1
16.	La Touche	37	7	60	6	56	3	44	1	40	3	3	1	242	1
17.	B. Vautro	-	-	48	3	23	2	50	2	49	6	27	2	198	5

Table 1. Results (M = Miles, L = Laps).[19]

Press coverage

Newspapers provided exciting day by day accounts of the races, but a few were critical. It inspired a satirical article that was originally published in *St James's Gazette*, which described the racing as 'the new (and particularly manly) British Sport'.[20] The article was later expanded

---

[17] *Sheffield Daily Telegraph*, November 27, 1896, 8; *The Standard*, November 16, 1895, 1; 'Bicycle Race for Ladies', *The New York Herald*, November 19, 1895, 1.

[18] Frivolets', *Fun*, December 3 1895, 1.

[19] *Sporting Life*, November 25, 1895 plus other articles. *Sporting Life* gave Rosina Lane a total of 343 miles and 3 laps with 57 miles and nine laps ridden on the final day, most other sources say 343 and 1 lap. The table has been adjusted based on majority reports. Of the 20 women, three riders abandoned the race on the first day and took no further part.

[20] 'Ladies and Laps', *St James's Gazette*, December 9, 1895, 5.

upon in *The Weekly Telegraph* as 'Ladies and Laps: A Satire on the Aquarium Cycling Show'. [21] It provided a humorous insight into attitudes to London's first women's six-day race, reflecting the mix of press viewpoints and featuring a mix of social classes and genders that attended the races. The spectator characters include a 'round-shouldered youth', who was there just to see how many of the racers crashed, evoking the kind of young person that moralists feared could be easily influenced into developing an unhealthy fascination with blood and violence. A virile bald-headed 'reprobate' shows more interest in the attractiveness of one rider than the racing, while a young doctor ponders the long-term health risks from cycling. The characters generally ridicule and criticise the racing, calling it 'revolting' and to be stopped by the police. Despite this, they still agree to return for the next race. The riders are depicted as typically fitting the views and debates regarding women during the period. One rider is described as fragile and in poor health, while one French rider is portrayed as masculine and uncouth, appearing in public smoking a cigar, swearing and dressed in men's clothing and a massive pair of bloomers. The newspaper *Fun* was critical that the women did not wear clothing that flattered their figures, stating: 'the costumes were disappointedly all round – absolutely round – and baggy. Same old pillow-cases, divided by two: so disappointing! We knew how *men* dressed […]. But the costumes were grim, and virtuous, and ugly – Chantesque in piety! [...] Even the shapely calves looked wan and weedy under those infernal, baggy sacks of 'knickers''.[22] The American cycling journal *The Referee & Cycle Trade Journal* was especially scornful, calling the event 'a disgusting exhibition' and describing the supposedly 'chic' French riders as having 'contorted faces, bent backs, hair fair flying wildly around their heads, their costumes soaked in certain spots where perspiration had oozed through'.[23]

The women of the race
Newspapers and the journals of the period generally provided scant information on the riders. Cycling-specific journals like *The Hub: An Illustrated Weekly for Wheelmen and Wheelwomen* published more in-depth illustrated interviews. Modern online digital archives and censuses now enable sports historians to build detailed profiles on these women racers for the first time in 120 years. The English riders are fairly

---

[21] 'Ladies and Laps: A Satire on the Aquarium Cycling Show', *The Weekly Telegraph*, December 21, 1895, 11.

[22] 'Frivolets', *Fun*, December 3, 1895, 1.

[23] 'A Disgusting Exhibition', *The Referee & Cycle Trade Journal*, December 19, 1895, 34.

uncomplicated to research, and some are profiled in this paper, but the French riders prove to be more difficult due to availability of online archival material and because the French press did little to actually profile their riders at the time, despite delivering a lot of coverage of the racing. As mentioned earlier, there were 20 women involved but only 17 riders finished the entire event.

This author has previously extensively researched and published papers on the French champion Lisette (real name Amélie Le Gall).[24] The other French riders – Gabrielle Etéogella, Nellie La Touche, Lucie Lutreille, Henriette Paillarde, Fanoche Vautro, the sisters Bèany and Marcelle Vautro, and Mademoiselles Cannoe, Solange, Reillo and Aboukaïa – are yet to be fully researched with little information to construct profiles based on genealogy research, racing careers and what they did after retiring. In the case of the latter rider, she did become much more famous after her cycling career, initially as an acrobat and eventually as a pioneering aviation pilot. Mlle Aboukaïa actually abandoned the first six-day race at the Royal Aquarium after the first day, taking no further part in the racing. The Vautro sisters, Marcelle and Bèany (real name Melanie Ann), were regulars at the Royal Aquarium races, as well as in France. They were born in Montluçon in central France in 1880 and 1878 respectively. Marcelle was the first of the French riders to race in Britain, having taken part in the women's cycle races during the summer of 1895.[25]

The English riders comprised Monica Harwood, Mrs Grace, Rosina Lane, Rosa Blackburn, Clara (or Clare) Gamble, Nellie Hutton, Lilian Adair and Miss Benham. Lilian Adair and Miss Benham withdrew on the first day and did not appear in any further cycle races after the first event in London, making them difficult to research. Miss Benham was actually pulled off the track 'on account of her erratic steering', after bringing down a number of riders.[26] There is little information on Miss Gamble, who finished seventh overall, but she continued racing at the Royal Aquarium up to 1897. If taking into consideration that all the English racers were based in and around the London area, the only

---

[24] Mike Fishpool, 'Mrs Grace versus Lisette: A Comparison of the English and French Women's Cycling Champions. Part 3: Lisette – The Women's Champion of France', *Playing Pasts*, May 9, 2019, http://www.playingpasts.co.uk; 'Lisette – France's Most Popular Lady Racer', *The Boneshaker*, Veteran-Cycle Club, Winter 2018, No 208, 24-34.

[25] Montluçon Baptisms 1877-1878/1879-1880 (2 E 191 74/77), Allier Departmental Archives, http://archives.allier.fr.

[26] 'Ladies Bicycle Races', *The Standard*, November 19, 1895, 6.

individual identified as a possible candidate for this rider was a Clara Jane Gamble, born in 1867 or 1868, who lived in Brentford.[27]

Mrs Clara Grace, who finished ninth, was profiled by this author for the *Playing Pasts* website in September 2018 and May 2019.[28] She was born Clara Simmons in Redbourn, Hertfordshire in 1865 and married William Grace in 1885, later relocating to Wood Green and bringing up four children (three daughters and one son). Clara started cycle racing in 1894 and was crowned the 'champion of England', gaining stature after she set women's endurance road records in 1895-1896. She went on to win races at the Royal Aquarium and Bingley Hall, Birmingham. After a bout of illness that prevented her from racing in 1897-1898, she retired from cycle racing in 1899.[29] Nellie Hutton was just 14 when she raced at the Royal Aquarium in November 1895, finishing in tenth position overall and was awarded a prize for the 'neatest costume'.[30] She was born Ellen Emma Hutton in 1881 in St Luke's, Middlesex and was the oldest of three children (two daughters and one son) belonging to William and Ellen Hutton living in Petherton Road in North London.[31] William ran a bicycle shop, also manufacturing his own bicycles under the 'Petherton' brand. It was one of these that Nellie raced on.[32] Her mother participated in several races in the summer 1895, coming up against Nellie a few times.[33] Nellie was a regular at the Royal Aquarium and had some successes in races held at the Olympia in West Kensington during 1896. She later married Edmund Henry Parnall in 1901. In the 1911 census, Nellie and Edmund Parnall were living in

[27] England, Wales & Scotland Census 1881, 1891, Findmypast, http://www.findmypast.co.uk.

[28] Mike Fishpool, September 10/17, 2018; 'Mrs Grace versus Lisette: A Comparison of the English and French Women's Cycling Champions. Part II: Mrs Grace – The Women's Champion of England', *Playing Pasts*, May 2, 2019, http://www.playingpasts.co.uk.

[29] 'Three Years as a Lady Racer. Some Experiences of Miss Blackburn', *The Hub*, March 12, 1898, 231.

[30] 'The Ladies' Race at the Royal Westminster Aquarium', *Sporting Life*, November 25, 1895, 1.

[31] England, Wales & Scotland Census 1891, 1901, 1911, Findmypast, http://www.findmypast.co.uk

[32] Chris Watts, *The Boneshaker*, 17; *The Hub*, March 20, 1897, 251-252.

[33] *Scottish Referee*, August 12, 1895, 4; *Glasgow Evening Post*, August 15, 1895, 6; *Greenock Telegraph and Clyde Shipping Gazette*, August 15, 1895, 4; 'Sports at the Manor Ground, Plumstead', *Kentish Mercury*, August 9, 1895, 6.

Ilford with four children (three daughters and one son) and one servant.[34]

The untold stories of three English riders

Monica Harwood came into professional women's cycling at just 18 years of age, beating the accomplished and much-admired French rider Lisette. Monica later became the captain of the Chelsea Rational Cycle Club (C.R.C.C.), which was formed in 1898 to promote rational dress for female cyclists and to undertake weekend club runs. Fellow cycle racer Rosina Lane was the club's honorary secretary and treasurer, while London-based rider Bèany Vautro was the vice-president. [35]

Monica Mary Harwood was born in 1878 in Buckingham. She was a

Fig 2. Monica Harwood, *The Hub*, 1898 (Modern Records Centre, University of Warwick).

farmer's daughter, the youngest of four children (two daughters and two son) belonging to William and Anne Harwood. In 1881, her mother was solely responsible for managing an entire farm of 132 acres in Northolt, Uxbridge in Middlesex, employing three men. The Harwood family relocated to a cottage in Twickenham by 1891 (minus one daughter and one son) and were joined by William Harwood, whose occupation was listed as a 'retired farmer'. The family relocated again around the time of Monica's cycle racing career to Staines Road, Bedfont in Middlesex, before Monica, her mother and two brothers moved by 1901 to Bulstrode Road, Hounslow.[36] Nicknamed 'Monie', Monica said in an interview in *The Hub* to have started cycling in July 1895 after being taught by one of her brothers and that it helped

---

[34] England, Wales & Scotland Census 1911; England & Wales Deaths 1837-2007 (Epping, Essex), Findmypast, http://www.findmypast.co.uk
[35] 'The Chelsea Rationalists', *The Hub*, July 9, 1898, 419
[36] England, Wales & Scotland Census 1881, 1891, 1901, Findmypast, http://www.findmypast.co.uk; 'A Chat with a Lady Speed Merchant. Miss Monica Harwood', *The Hub*, March 26, 1898, 297.

improve her health, having been in 'delicate health' a few years previously.[37] *The Queen: The Lady's Newspaper* stated that she started racing shortly after taking to the wheel under the direction of Clara Grace.[38] Monica raced upon a 10.4 kg (23 lb) 'Elysee' racing bicycle equipped with Dunlop pneumatic tyres but switched to Symonds Roberts' Royal Racer towards the end of her racing career.[39] She would train on the road and track for 'two to three hours', two weeks before a race with a preference for paced 50 and 100-mile races. Her first race was in Hull in the summer 1895, an experience that led her to remark that: 'it was the very first time I had seen a proper track. The high banking quite frightened me, and I imagine it would never be possible to ride round safely. However, I started, and I managed to come third in a two-mile race'.[40] She was one of the main British stars of the track, racing in London at the Royal Aquarium, Newcastle, Sheffield, Southampton and Paris.[41]

Monica was among one of four riders participating in a specially organized event at the Royal Agricultural Hall in early 1896 that built on the first Royal Aquarium race. It was held to match the best of the English and French women riders with Monica racing one-on-one against the Belgian-born Hélène Dutrieux in a paced 50-mile race on 23 March, which she lost, and coming second and third in a further 50-mile race on 28 March, separated into two 25-mile races that also involved Dutrieux, Mrs Grace and Gabrielle Etéogella.[42] Monica was also among the five women competitors who took part in one-mile races at the Royal Aquarium in January-February 1899, riding on static bicycles on stage – she participated in further static races at the Tivoli Variety Theatre in Glasgow in October that year.[43] Her last races at the Royal Aquarium were a series of sixes held on 3-29 June 1901 before the venue shut its

---

[37] 'A Lady Champ Who Rides a Man's Bicycle', *The Hub*, August 22, 1896, 120; 'A Chat with a Lady Speed Merchant. Miss Monica Harwood', *The Hub*, March 26, 1898, 297.

[38] *The Queen: The Lady's Newspaper*, December 7, 1895, 1095.

[39] Chris Watts, 'The Royal Aquarium and Summer and Winter Garden, Westminster', *The Boneshaker*, Summer 2007, No 174, 17; 'Once upon a time or your perfect bike (especially for the Gentle Ladies)?', Fossilcycle, https://fossilcycle.wordpress.com.

[40] 'A Chat with a Lady Speed Merchant. Miss Monica Harwood', *The Hub*, March 26, 1898, 297.

[41] *Newcastle Courant*, January 4, 1896, 4; *Sporting Life*, February 4, 1899, 2; *Sporting Life*, May 6, 1899, 7.

[42] *London Evening Standard*, March 24, 1896, 3; *South Wales Daily News*, March 31, 1896, 7.

[43] *Sporting Life*, January, 24, 1899, 4; October, 2, 1899, 8.

doors for the last time, eventually being demolished to make way for the Methodist Central Hall. Monica came second in the first race on 3-8 June, which featured five riders from the first event six years earlier amongst the 12 competitors, and she won a second six-day race on 10-15 June.[44] On 19 October 1901, she established a British women's hour record at Putney Velodrome of 24 miles and 780 yards (713 metres), paced by tandems and beating the record that she had previously set.[45] Monica was then reported in March 1902 performing on a small track on stage with two men and another woman named Emilie Golding, who had also taken part in the Royal Aquarium races the previous summer. This group were known as 'Ransley Troupe', which was formed in 1899 and managed by a 'Madame E. Ransley'. It performed at the London Pavilion that month. [46] Monica also assisted a 'Madame Lizette' (presumably not the same French rider who was based in the US at the time) racing on a mini track on the stage of the Osborne Theatre in Manchester in August 1902. Further adverts detail 'Madame Lizette's Cycling Sensation on the Teacup Track – The smallest and steepest track in the world. 120 laps to the mile' and 'Mdme Lizette's lady cycling sensation, in which a troupe of five cyclists, two of whom are males, give a daring display on a 'teacup' track. The track is sloped at an angle of 65 degrees'.[47] With no further reports of Monica's involvement in these performances after 1902, it can be presumed that she had retired. She married William John Collingham five years later, eventually living in Lambeth where William was employed as a hotel waiter, and raised two sons, William and Norman. Monica Collingham died in 1961 at the grand old age of 83.[48]

Rosina Lane finished in sixth position in the first six-day race at the Royal Aquarium and was one of two racing mothers, along with Clara Grace. It was her costume that *The Manchester Guardian* had called 'the ugliest' in its coverage of the racing, featuring an innovative skirt designed by Rosina's sister-in-law Alice Bygrave and marketed for

---

[44] *Lancashire Evening Post*, June 10, 1901, 6; *Sporting Life*, June 17, 1901, 1.

[45] *Sporting Life*, November 6, 1901, 2.

[46] *The Era*, April 29, 1899, 21; *Music Hall and Theatre Review*, April 4, 1902, 1; *The Stage*, March 2, 1905, 1.

[47] *Greenock Telegraph and Clyde Shipping Gazette*, January 23, 1902, 1; *Dublin Evening Telegraph*, April 7, 1902, 1; *Edinburgh Evening News*, December 23, 1902, 2.

[48] England, Wales & Scotland Census 1911, England & Wales births 1837-2006, Findmypast, http://www.findmypast.co.uk.

general cycling and walking use as the 'Bygrave Convertible Skirt'.[49] Her full name was Amelia Rosina Lane and she was born in 1860 in Standish, Gloucestershire. Rosina was one of nine children (four girls, five boys) belonging to James and Elizabeth Lane. In the 1861 census, James was working as a farm bailiff managing 65 acres of land in the Standish area with Ann plus Rosina, three other daughters and two sons; the Lane family expanded with three further sons born in 1861-1868. Ann, Rosina and two sisters plus her five brothers moved to Aston in Warwickshire by 1871 without James (he may have been working in Straiton, Ayrshire in Scotland as a hay baler). Ann, Rosina, and two sons then moved to Chelsea by 1881 where Rosina, aged 21, was working as a machinist. She subsequently married Arthur George Duerre in 1883, a watchmaker by trade, and the couple had relocated by 1891 to 190 Kings Road, Chelsea where they ran a watchmaking and jewellery shop with two daughters, Lilian and Winifred. Rosina had two further daughters in 1892-1894, Alma and Gladys. In the 1911 census, Rosina and the youngest daughter Gladys assisted Arthur in the shop in Kings Road, as well as having a servant and a granddaughter named Lily Bee living with them.[50]

It appears that the Royal Aquarium event was Rosina's first foray into cycle racing. Arthur Duerre may have been an influence; he was a member of the Chelsea Bicycle and Tricycle Club (Chelsea B&T.C.) and had participated in club races from 1892.[51] Rosina returned for further races at the Royal Aquarium, the Olympia and Birmingham up to 1898. She primarily rode in handicap races and also appears to have ridden as part of a professional pacing team belonging to the Coventry-based Swift Cycle Company. An image of her on a triplet was published in the journal *The Sketch* in 1895 with Rosa Blackburn and another rider named Miss Murray.[52] In her role as the honorary secretary of the C.R.C.C. with her home acting as the club's 'town' headquarters (Monica Harwood's Bedfont home was the 'country' headquarters), Rosina organized an open international race at Putney Velodrome on 15 August 1898 with the club's president, Mrs Chaundy.[53] The race provided an opportunity to display rational dress and according to a report on the event in

---

[49] Kat Jungnickel, *Bikes and Bloomers: Victorian Women Inventors and their Extraordinary Cycle Wear* (London: Goldsmiths University of London, 2018), 121-154.

[50] England, Wales & Scotland Census 1861, 1871, 1881, 1891, 1901, 1911, Findmypast, http://www.findmypast.co.uk.

[51] *Sporting Life*, July 6, 1892, 3; *London Daily News*, August 20, 1897, 3.

[52] Dick Swan, 'Early Women Racers', *The Boneshaker*, Spring 1992, No 128, 13; Kat Jungnickel, *Bikes and Bloomers*, 135.

[53] 'The Chelsea Rationalists', *The Hub*, July 9, 1898, 419.

Sporting Life the next day, most of the spectators had originally attended to see Monica Harwood and another rider named Mrs Scott, but neither made the start line. Rosina rode an 'exhibition mile' paced by a triplet, while her daughter Lilian rode her first races that included coming second in a one-mile 'skirts v rational dress' scratch race.[54] Rosina's cycling career came to an abrupt end six days after the Putney Velodrome race when she was struck by a horse and carriage whilst cycling in Richmond Park. It led her to go to court to recover damages, being awarded £55. The court case report stated that her 'bicycle was smashed, the "rational costume" in which she was riding was torn to pieces'.[55]

This was not the first time that Rosina would end up in court. Indeed, she had previously been fined for 'scorching' (riding at speeds perceived to be too fast for public highways) in Kingston, London and

Fig 3. Rosina Lane, *The Hub*, 1898 (Modern Records Centre, University of Warwick).

in March 1897, she unsuccessfully tried in Westminster County Court to seek damages from the Royal Aquarium for lost wages.[56] At start of the twentieth century, Rosina was again in the public eye but for all the wrong reasons. In September 1909, Rosina and Arthur were fined a total of £130 for running an illegal betting house in their Kings Road shop. The *Gloucestershire Echo* said: 'It was stated that a very large business was done, and that the premises – a jeweller's shop – were fitted up with tapes and telephones'.[57] The couple's messy separation that was being pursued through the courts was also played out publicly in various newspapers in 1914-1916 with additional reports during the period

---

[54] 'The Chelsea Rational Cycling Club: Good Sport by Lady Riders', *Sporting Life*, August 16, 1898, 4.

[55] 'Professional Lady Cyclist's Spill', *The Daily Telegraph*, March 9, 1899, 4.

[56] 'Lady Cyclist's Earnings', *Reynolds's Newspaper*, March 7, 1897, 8; Kat Jungnickel, *Bikes and Bloomers*, 134.

[57] *Gloucestershire Echo*, September 11, 1909, 1.

suggesting that it was a very traumatic period in their lives.[58] Rosina died in 1938, aged 78.[59]

Rosa Blackburn finished eighth at the Royal Aquarium in November 1895, stating that 'I had terribly bad luck. The track was strange to me, and I had well over a dozen falls, in two of which I ran right up the banking and fell over amongst the people'. Perhaps learning from the experience, she went on to win a 25-mile handicap race at the venue in the same month.[60]

Fig. 4. Rosa Blackburn, *The Hub*, 1898 (Modern Records Centre, University of Warwick).

Rosa was born in 1878 in Islington, Middlesex, one of seven children (five daughters and two sons) belonging to Henry Blackburn, a railway signalman, and his wife Annie. The family lived at 12 Hatley Road, Islington.[61] Rosa started racing in the cycling tour in July-August 1895 and then at Woolwich Arsenal F.C'.s Manor Ground, Plumstead on 5 August where she won a half-mile race beating both Nellie Hutton and her mother in the final heat in front of up to 4,000 spectators. She also raced against Nellie's younger sister Maud (then aged 7!) as well as a Parisian rider in the second heat of this race. [62] After the first twelve-day race, Rosa then rode in Birmingham, at the Olympia and continued to race at the Royal Aquarium, winning overall in December 1896. In eight weeks of racing at the Royal Aquarium at

---

[58] 'Chelsea Tradesman's Grave Injury', *Chelsea News and General Advertiser*, July 31, 1914, 5; 'King's Road Woman Incapable', February 5, 1915, 2; 'Jeweller's Shop Problem', March 24, 1916, 3. *West London Press*, January 16, 1914; March 10, 1916;

[59] England & Wales Deaths 1837-2007 (Battersea, London), Findmypast, http://www.findmypast.co.uk.

[60] *London Evening Standard*, November 29, 1895, 3.

[61] England, Wales & Scotland Census 1881, 1891, 1901, Findmypast, http://www.findmypast.co.uk

[62] 'Sports at the Manor Ground, Plumstead', *Kentish Mercury*, August 9, 1895, 6.

the end of 1896, Rosa rode 3,049 miles, taking a salary and winnings of £140. She won three further sixes and 12-day races at the Royal Aquarium in January and June 1897. At some point, her success enabled her to be crowned the women's 'champion of England', succeeding Clara Grace. She also participated in races at the Royal Agricultural Hall, in Southampton and Paris.[63]

In April 1899, Rosa took part in women's races that were being held as part of a gala and 'Olympian entertainment' held at Balmoral, Belfast in Northern Ireland where she represented England against three other women representing the 'champions' of the home nations.[64] She also organized a race the following month at the Putney Velodrome where she rode against a male runner named Harry Hutchens and won a tandem pursuit with Monica Harwood.[65] Rosa started her early racing career riding a Swift racing bicycle but later switched to 'Triumph' bike.[66] She promoted Elliman's Universal Embrocation, an ointment for muscles and joints made out of eggs, vinegar and turpentine, mirroring Clara Grace who regularly recommended the similar St Jacob's Oil in newspaper advertisements.[67] Rosa was one of the few women to continue racing after major professional women's cycle racing ended. After winning a six-day race at the Royal Aquarium on 3-8 June 1901 and coming second to Monica Harwood at the venue a week later, she returned to Balmoral Park again in August, racing in several short races and providing a three-mile exhibition race. She then switched to the Tee-To-Tum Athletic Grounds at Stamford Hill, London to take part in women's races in August and October 1901, and again in May 1902, setting a women's one-lap record at both events in 1901.[68] Her last races took place at the Recreation Ground, Great Yarmouth on 3 August 1903. The event, which may have been the last professional women's track races until several decades later, involved six riders in one and three-mile scratch races – some of whom had been regulars at the Royal

---

[63] 'Three Years as a Lady Racer. Some Experiences of Miss Blackburn', *The Hub*, March 12, 1898, 231; *Penny Illustrated Paper*, June 12, 1897, 10; *Hampshire Advertiser*, June 23, 1897, 2; *Islington Gazette*, May 27, 1898, 2; Six-Day Cycle Races, http://www.sixday.org.uk.

[64] *Belfast News-Letter*, April 4, 1899, 6.

[65] *Sporting Life*, May 8, 1899, 3.

[66] *The Hub*, March 20, 1897, 251; Dick Swan, 'Early Women Racers', *The Boneshaker*, Spring 1992, No 128, 13.

[67] *Driffield Times*, April 23, 1898, 4; 'Mrs Clara Grace, The Champion Lady Rider', *Illustrated London News*, November 27, 1897, 26.

[68] *Belfast News-Letter*, August 5, 1901, 3; *Sporting Life*, September 4, 1901, 7; *Sporting Life*, October 5, 1901, 6; *Tyrone Courier*, October 10, 1901, 7; *Sporting Life*, May 21, 1902, 1.

Aquarium and at other major races a few years earlier.[69] Rosa married Francis James Meddings in 1902; Frank Meddings also dabbled in cycle racing and in 1901 was living at Hatley Road with the Blackburn family – he was listed as an 'estate superintendent'. The couple had by 1911 moved to Harringay where Frank was working as an assistant estate foreman while Rosa brought up two daughters, Gladys and Evelyn Rosa. Rosa Meddings passed away in 1929, aged 51.[70]

[69] *Norfolk News*, August 8, 1903, 6.
[70] England, Wales & Scotland Census 1901, 1911, Marriages and Deaths (Wandsworth, London), Findmypast, http://www.findmypast.co.uk.

5

Jack Price and the 1908 Olympic Marathon

Luke Harris

Abstract

The 1908 Olympic Marathon is one of the most written about events in Modern Olympic History, with the main protagonists being the feature of many articles and chapters. Almost absent from this extensive histography is a detailed explanation about the performance of the eleven British athletes that began the race. This chapter's intention is to begin to undercover the story of one of the British athletes, Jack Price, a resident of Halesowen, Worcestershire and a representative of Small Heath Harriers from Birmingham. Like so many of the British team, Price was selected following his performance in one of the Olympic Trial Races run in the Spring of 1908. This race will be analysed, as will his preparations for the Olympic Marathon, which demonstrate the slightly haphazard organisation behind Britain's athletic organization for the 1908 Olympics. A range of sources will be examined to explain the reasons why not only Jack Price but all of the British athletes failed in this pivotal Olympic event.

Keywords: Olympic Games, Marathon, Athletics, Jack Price, Birmingham.

Introduction

The 1908 Olympic Marathon remains perhaps the most infamous race in Olympic History. The victory and subsequent disqualification of the Italian athlete Dorando Pietri created an excitement and legacy that propelled this relatively new event to the forefront of athletics. Pietri's disqualification and the awarding of the race to the Irish-American Johnny Hayes following a gruelling battle on the streets of North and West London is a well-told story.[1] Comparatively, there is little written about the fate of any of the twelve athletes who represented Britain in this race. These men, at least in the eyes of the British press, were amongst the favourites for the race, although none of them featured in

---

[1] Accounts of the race appear in amongst others; John Bryant, *26.2: The Incredible True Story of the Three Men who Shaped the London Marathon* (London: John Blake, 2013), David Davis, *Showdown in Shepherd's Bush* (New York: Thomas Dunne, 2012), Rebecca Jenkins, *The First London Olympics: 1908* (London: Piaktus, 2012)

the final reckoning owing to a combination of injury, the heat and perhaps most significantly; inexperience. This chapter will begin to explore this relatively unknown tale via the examination of one of the British athletes; Jack Price, who represented the Birmingham athletic club Small Heath Harriers, and was one of Britain's leading hopes following his victory in the Midlands Marathon Trial of May 1908.

Background

John (Jack) Price was born in Neen Savage, Shropshire on 18 February 1884. It was in this rural setting that he remained until the age of 16, when after he had grown tired of tending sheep and cattle on a farm he 'set out to seek a new world', and after a day's walking he arrived at the town of Halesowen, located in the area affectionately known as the 'Black Country', on a 'hot, dusty, July evening'[2] in 1901. Price soon found himself a job with local steel makers, Stewarts and Lloyds, and remained in the town for the rest of his life.

It was not for another three years, by which time Price was 'married and blessed with a bonnie daughter',[3] that his athletic career began. This came during a walking race between Halesowen and Kidderminster, in which he only competed following an invitation from a friend. After an unremarkable start, he found himself ninth at the halfway stage, five minutes behind the leaders. In the second half of the race, Price's position improved and a strong finish ensured that he finished second and 'a few yards behind a man named Walters'.[4] This is the first evidence of the strong finish which was to become his trademark, and was good enough for Price to win the race, allowing for his handicap of five minutes.

This initial success encouraged Price to compete in a range of athletic contests over the following year. Race walking remained at the forefront of his activities. He also ventured into running, competing in mile races during the summer and cross-country running, the staple of the athletics in the West Midlands, in the winter. Price quickly developed a particular passion for cross-country, aided by the Client Hills which lay to the South-West of his adopted home and provided an excellent training ground. In order to compete in more cross-country events, he

---

[2] 'Jack Price', *Halesowen Athletic & Cycling Club, 1922-1949: Official Opening of the Manor Abbey Sports Ground*, (August 1949), 29.
[3] Jack Price, 'My experiences across country', *The Stagbearer* 7, No 1, (1932), 3.
[4] Ibid.

joined the Cradley Heath branch of the Birmingham-based athletics club Small Heath Harriers in late 1905.[5]

From this point onwards, Price established himself as an excellent cross-country runner, and in the spring of 1906, he competed in the English National Championships at Haydock Park for the first time. Price later commented that 'this race will always remain vividly impressed on my memory, for at the end of first lap my position was 43rd, and at the finish (I was) seventh'.[6] This race provided yet further evidence of Price's strong finish and it earned him selection in the England team for the 'International' Cross-Country Championship at Caerleon, which featured athletes from the four 'home' nations and France; Price was to finish in a respectable seventh position.[7]

Fig. 1. Jack Price in action.

Price's growing reputation was further enhanced by an interview for the *Athletic News* in January 1907, which described him as a 'tall, angular man' and 'a real, straightforward amateur, a splendid club man,'[8] and made reference to his real strength. That Spring his growing reputation within English cross-country running was demonstrated by his selection for the 'International', despite his absence from the English National Championships because of a bout of influenza.[9] In the

---

[5] Ibid.

[6] Ibid

[7] 'Cross-Country and Athletic Topics', *Athletic News*, 28 January 1907, 3.

[8] Ibid.

[9] Pleader, 'Cross-Country and Athletic Topics: The Midlands', *Athletic News*, 11 March 1907, 3.

'International', Price finished a disappointing tenth, owing to a foot injury, a position he was to replicate during the AAA Ten-Mile Championships the following month. [10] Price's performances had helped established him as an international quality runner, but there was little indication of the success that was to follow.

The summer of 1907 appears to be a pivotal period in Price's development. Following victory in his preferred summer event; the mile, at the Crusader Harriers Annual Event, the *County Advertiser & Herald for Staffordshire and Worcestershire* commented that he 'seems to have found what he has long needed - a little pace'.[11] This performance came shortly after his first victories in a mile race at West Smethwick and a three-mile handicap at Villa Park, following a 'most determined effort in the last two laps'.[12] These results indicate that Price had found some pace, a valuable asset in his future successes.

Marathon Runner
During the spring of 1908, like so many of the premier distance runners in Britain, Price turned his attention to an unfamiliar event to English eyes, the Marathon. The event had become a highlight of the Olympic Games since its inception twelve years previously, but it had not taken off in Britain. The reason for this potentially was the preference for sprint and middle-distance races in Edwardian athletic meetings which produced more frequent moments of drama in order to satisfy the demands of the paying punter. The consequence of this had been that in the four previous Olympic Marathons (if the 1906 Intercalated Games are included), Britain had provided only six competitors and only James Cormack had completed the race in 1906, finishing in fourteenth place, 44 minutes behind the winner, Billy Sherring of Canada.[13]

The lack of knowledge about the Marathon, and who Britain's representatives might be, ensured that in order to select their twelve representatives, the Amateur Athletic Association (AAA) sanctioned a series of Marathon trial races to be held across the country during the Spring of 1908. This approach was totally different compared to that for

---

[10] A.E. Machin, 'Athletic Notes: Midlands who didn't score', *Sport and Play and Wheel Life*, 30 March 1907, 12. 'The Midland Brigade', *Sport and Play and Wheel Life*, 20 April 1907, 14.

[11] 'Sporting Items', *County Advertiser & Herald for Staffordshire and Worcestershire*, 8 June 1907, 7.

[12] 'Wolseley A.C. Sports: J. Price the hero of the three miles race', *Athletic News*, 22 July 1907, 2.

[13] Martin Polley, 'From Windsor Castle to White City: The 1908 Olympic Marathon Route', *The London Journal* 34, No 2, (2009), 168

the other track and field events, where athletes were selected following a single trial, held at the White City Stadium, the location of the Olympic Track and Field meeting, including the conclusion of the Marathon.

In total, there were eight 'Marathons' run during April and May 1908 (some of the distances varied, with some of the races taking place over just 20 miles). Three of these races were considered the 'official' Marathon trials and sanctioned by the AAA, and were held in Manchester, London and Birmingham (organized by Salford Harriers, Polytechnic Harries and Birchfield Harriers respectively), and the majority of the British Marathon athletes were selected based on their performance in these races. Detailed accounts of these races can be found in the *The Marathon Race* and *The Manchester Marathons*.[14]

The first official trial took place on 21 March 1908 and was organized by Salford Harriers. There is no evidence of Jack Price ever intending to run in this race, but he was amongst the 80 entrants for the London trial, held over much of the Olympic course on 25 April. Despite leaving Halesowen early that Saturday morning, a missed train connection ensured that he failed to make the start on time.[15] This meant that his only chance to impress the selectors came in his 'home' Marathon trial, that began in Coventry and finished at the Hawthorns, the home of West Bromwich Albion Football Club. The race had first been mentioned by Birchfield club secretary W.W. Alexander on 15 January 1908, where he described the request to organize the race as an 'honour'[16] and over the coming months two routes were mentioned as possibilities, with that from Worcester to Birmingham the favourite, although at the last minute the alternative route between Coventry and West Bromwich was chosen.[17]

In total there were 31 entries in the race, twelve of whom came from Birchfield; with another six from Bearwood Harriers, while Price was amongst the six men representing Small Heath Harriers. Price stated that, 'for this race I had no particular training except one run on the road, about twenty miles, a fortnight before'.[18] His final preparations

---

[14] David E. Martin and Roger W.H. Gynn, *The Marathon Footrace*, (Illinois: Charles C Thomas, 1979). Ron Hill and Neil Shuttleworth, *Manchester Marathons*, 1908-2002, (Dublin: Litho, 2003)

[15] W.W. Alexander, 'Athletic Notes', *Sporting Mail*, 11 May 1908, 1.

[16] W.W. Alexander, 'Olympic Games', 15 January 1908 (Birchfield Harriers Archives).

[17] A.E. Machin, 'Athletic Notes: The Birchfield 'Marathon' race', *Sport and Play and Wheel Life*, 4 April 1908, 14-15.

[18] Jack Price, 'My Marathon Experiences', *The Stagbearer* 8. Vol 1, (1932) 3.

were made all the more difficult by working 'till midnight at the furnaces of Combs Wood Works'[19] the evening before the Marathon. The favourite for the race was the veteran Dido Day of Birchfield Harriers. He was a frequent adversary of Price on the cross-country circuit and had experience of 'Marathon' running, having unsuccessfully run in the Salford Harriers trial race in March.[20] Price stated that Day had undertaken a full trial on the course, and 'twas said whoever beat Dido would win'.[21]

An article in the Birmingham weekly the *Sporting Mail* described the forthcoming race:

> An excellent course of 25 miles had been mapped out, beginning at the railway bridge on the main road between Allesley and Coventry, and ending at the Albion football ground at West Bromwich, where the Birchfield club ran a sports meeting in conjunction with the trial…A challenge cup, value £25, was offered for competition, to be held by the winning team for 12 months, and there were four gold medals for the leading members, with silver and bronze medals respectively for teams-four to count-placed second and third. Competitors were permitted to run only the turnpike road, and pace-making was prohibited'.[22]

There was also the thought that the distance of the race at 25 miles (making it the longest of the eight trials), along with its hilly terrain, made this the toughest of the eight Marathon trials held. A report of the race described a crowd of 'about 4,000' being present for the start at 3:06 pm and that the course was littered with spectators and 'at least 1,000 cyclists' [23] were present at Stonebridge for the runner's' arrival. Stonebridge marked the eight-mile mark in the race, and here it was the Birchfield athlete Stamps led, while a chasing group, which included Day and Price were nearly 300 yards behind. Stamps' lead lasted until just beyond the 16-mile mark, when Price took the lead:

> On the way to Castle Bromwich Stamps gave way the head of affairs to Price, who went through the village at a good swinging

---

[19] 'Jack Price's Career: He won the Powderhall Marathon', *Sports Argus*, 28 May 1949, 3.
[20] W.W. Alexander, 'Athletic Notes', *Sporting Mail*, 4 April 1908, 1.
[21] Jack Price, 'My Marathon Experiences', *The Stagbearer* 8. Vol 1, (1932) 3.
[22] Athletics: Great Road race: Birchfield Marathon Trial', *Sporting Mail*, 4 May 1908, 2.
[23] Ibid.

pace, with Day 1min 53 sec behind. Two and a half minutes later nipped by, followed by Lewis, between whom and the leader there was an interval of 5min 15 sec...A host of cyclists were hanging on to the heels of the leader (Price). The Small Heath man was nearly a mile in front of Day at Tyburn House. At Beggar's Bush (18 miles), Price was leading 1½ miles from Day.[24]

Price continued to build his lead, and he passed the finish line at the Hawthorns 17 minutes 27 seconds ahead of the second-placed Day. Following his triumph, Price received a gold medal from Harry Butler of the MCAAA to 'to mark what was regarded as an outstanding performance'. [25] Despite the manner of the victory, Price was disappointed to have finished just outside the 25 mile amateur record set by G.A. Dunning in 1881, a record which Price would attempt to beat on two separate occasions during 1909.

Following the victory, the press was full of plaudits for Price's performance. In the *Athletic News*, Pleader explained that:

I have Price's word for it that he never had a bad time in the race and was in good condition up to twenty-two miles. Thereabouts, the vibration affected his legs below the knee, and for a mile he was 'groggy'. But those who saw his memorable finish will need no assurance as to his condition when the 25 ½ miles were ended. He finished the freshest man in the race.[26]

Birmingham sporting periodical *Sport and Play and Wheel Life*, described Price's performance as 'super-excellent,' and that it was 'the performance of the day, dwarfing all others, and comparison with the best performances in the races that have preceded it must certainly be accorded a high value'.[27] The article explained that after covering the first ten miles in 58m 33s, Price opened a small gap over Day, and that 'the further Price went, the longer his lead became' and at fifteen miles he sprinted up the 'stiff hill' near Tyburn House and with it making his lead up to 'about a mile in front', by the twenty mile mark his lead had extended to 11 ½ minutes and by the finish he was 17m 27s ahead, 'a gain of six minutes in the last five miles'.

---

[24] Ibid.

[25] Jack Price, 'My Marathon Experiences', *The Stagbearer* 8. Vol 1, (1932) 3.

[26] Pleader, 'A Midland Star: John Price, Small Heath Harrier', *Athletic News*, 29 June 1908, 2.

[27] 'Athletic Notes: The Midland Marathon Race', *Sport and Play and Wheel Life*, 16 May 1908, 14.

Place	Name	Club	Time
1	J. Price	Small Heath	2.37.13
2	W.H. Day	Birchfield	2.54.40
3	A. Edwards	Small Heath	2.56.45
4	A.F. Lewis	Birchfield	3.0.23
5	S.T. Smith	Birchfield	3.8.14
6	A.W. Soley	Bearwood	3.17.19
7	A.R. Cutler	Bearwood	3.27.12
8	D.R. O'Donovan	Finchley	3.28.41
9	E.Mountenary	Birchfield	3.29.43
10	W. Mountenary	Birchfield	3.30.54
11	W. Mounterary	Birchfield	3.34.9
12	P.W. Tippitis	Bearwood	3.34.9
13	J.H. Whitworth	Small Heath	3.42.58
14	S. Price	Bearwood	3.44.58
15	A. Giles	Small Heath	3.54.17
16	W.H. Honk	Small Heath	3.55.14
17	W.Pitts	Birchfield	3.56.23
18	W.H. Edwards	Birchfield	4.28.03

Table 1: Full Result of the Midland Olympic Trial.[28]

Reflecting on the race in his weekly column in the *Sporting Mail*; W.W. Alexander described the race as 'without doubt the most severe test' of all the trial races and he believed that there 'should be little trouble in finding a place for the winner, J. Price, in the British team at the big Olympic Games'. Alexander did worry that in the eyes of the 'London critics', they might not see it as an equal to the victory of Duncan in the Polytechnic trial, but believed his performance was at least 'on a par' with it, and if Price had competed in the Polytechnic trial 'he must have been right up with Duncan, if not he had beaten him'. He concluded that:

> No doubt the conditions under which the competitors ran in the Southern race had some effect on the time, but the course on Saturday was fully three miles farther, and the hilly roads, with long climb at the finish, made the Midland course much the harder of the two, so that on time Price can claim to be well in the running for a road record. The committee must take this into consideration when finally selecting the team.[29]

---

[28] Ibid.
[29] W.W. Alexander, 'Athletic Notes', *Sporting Mail*, 11 May 1908, 1.

The reference to the conditions at the Polytechnic, referred to the slush and mud – following a snowfall - which were endured during parts of the race.[30] The British Marathon entrants were due to be named in early June following the track and field trials on 30 May.

Fig. 2. Jack Price's medal from the Midland Marathon Trial.[31]

Price's preparations for the Olympic marathon

Despite Alexander's concerns about Price's possible omission, the Midland Marathon Trial runner was named amongst the twelve British athletes selected for the Olympic marathon. Alongside the sprinter John Morton, they were the only representatives selected for track and field from the West Midlands. The selection did not bring with it any formal pre-games training, and all the British athletes were left to their own devices to prepare. Consequently, Price's club, Small Heath Harriers, began fundraising to enable him to undertake extra training. Their primary means of fundraising came via an appeal made to local athletic clubs. The following letter is the letter that was sent to fellow Birmingham athletic club Birchfield Harriers in May 1908:

> Dear Sir,
>
> No doubt you are aware that one of our members J. Price the winner of the recent Midland Marathon Race has been honoured

---

[30] 'The Polytechnic Marathon Trial Race', *The Polytechnic Magazine*, May 1908, 41
[31] Published with permission of Jack Price's grandson, Mick Whitehead.

by being selected to represent this country in the forthcoming 25 Miles Marathon race in connection with the Olympic Games, which take place at the Stadium next month, he being the only Birmingham representative in this event.

It has been considered desirable that J. Price should undergo a special course of training, in order to be thoroughly fit for this important race, to enable him to compete under equal conditions with the specially-trained athletes representing the various countries from all parts of the world; but a preparation of this kind, which is most essential for such an arduous task, will necessarily entail considerable expenses and, owing to lack of funds, the Club find it impossible to render him the financial assistance that would be necessary. Therefore, a Subscription List has been opened with this subject in view, and seeing that this particular race is a matter of such national importance, on behalf of the Committee, I earnestly appeal to you kindly favour us with your financial support.

Thanking you in anticipation,

Yours faithfully,

Chas. C. Linton, Hon. Sec.[32]

The tone of this letter gives some suggestion that Small Heath were not in such a fortunate financial position that they alone could support Price's preparations. Such training certainly was opposite to the values of 'effortless superiority' favoured by those administering English athletics, suggesting a Midland athletic identity more in-line with that favoured in the North of England than the south. The location at which the letter was found indicates that Birchfield were one of the clubs approached to contribute to the fund, although no confirmation of that can be found. One organization that donated to Price's fund was the Midland Counties Amateur Athletic Association (MCAAA), which gave £5 5s.[33]

There is no other indication that the MCAAA aided Price's preparations apart from to give him (and the other athletes selected to represent Britain under their jurisdiction) their train fare to enable them to reach

---

[32] Letter written by Charles. C. Linton, (Small Heath Harriers) to Birchfield Harriers. (Birchfield Harriers Archive).

[33] Midland Counties Amateur Athletic Association, 7 May 1908.

London for their event.[34] Reporting on the fundraising, the *Athletic News* indicated that raising money for Midland athletes only arose following a notion with 'particular reference to the Small Heath Harrier, J. Price'.[35] An editorial in *Sport and Play and Wheel Life* explained that there was apathy towards this appeal:

> There does not seem the desire that was thought existed to subscribe to the found being raised to provide the only Midland honoured with a place in the Marathon Race with a little special training but I think that can only be because it has not been brought to the notice of a good many sportsmen. I am of in receipt of 2s.6d. from Mr D. Lucas, of Kettering, for the Price Fund, and that gentleman sends his mite as 'An admirer of the way Price has always run for his club'. There must be many other sportsmen about who will help such a good cause, and I trust to hear from some of them during the week.[36]

The *Athletic News* gave further insight into Price's preparations in an article entitled 'A Midland Star: John Price'. It began by stating the importance of the marathon race, explaining it was the 'greatest concern' of the forthcoming Olympics, before describing his performance in the Midlands trial race and a quote from Price where he explained his preparations. Price stated he was, 'having a week from work…just to get strong; and then I go back for a week and then another week's holiday will bring the race along'. The article continued by explaining that would be the 'the extent of Price's training and it is to the credit of his club, the Small Heather Harriers, that even that moderate abstention from arduous labour has been possible. For Price, being a stoker, does really earn his bread by the sweat of his brow'.[37]

Birmingham's 'pink-un', the *Sports Argus* further elaborated on Price's preparations, explaining that the first of these weeks was spent in the Worcestershire town of Pershore, where he trained with the Small Heath Club trainer, J. Duggan. Duggan was not Price's normal trainer, as Harry Jones, a Halesowen resident and close friend of Price's had helped him prepare for the Birchfield Marathon, but for reasons that are

---

[34] E W Cox, 'Note and anecdote', *Sporting Mail*, 1 August 1908, 2.

[35] Pleader, 'Racing afoot and a wheel: The Midlands', *Athletic News*, 22 June 1908, 6.

[36] 'Athletic Notes: The Olympic Training Fund', *Sport and Play and Wheel Life*, 28 June 1908, 14.

[37] Pleader, 'A Midland Star: John Price, Small Heath Harrier', *Athletic News*, 29 June 1908, 2.

unclear, he was not permitted by the Small Heath Committee to administer his preparations for the Olympic Marathon.[38]

Price's Olympic marathon

The marathon race was undoubtedly the blue-ribbon event of the 1908 Olympics, coming on the penultimate day of athletic competition. The press gave the race extensive coverage; for example, *The Times* preview even included a map of the course.[39]

There appears to be several factors behind the interest in this race; primarily the uniqueness of the race and the stamina it required. For the British, the marathon represented an opportunity to prove their physical prowess, a notion that had been questioned since the press picked up on the recruitment issues for the British Army to fight in the Boer War (1899) and one furthered in the decade since by other factors, including international sporting defeats.[40] At the 1908 Olympics, success in the marathon became of even greater importance to the British following the dominance of the American athletes during the track and field meeting, where prior to the marathon they had won twelve gold medals over eleven days of competition (which would increase to sixteen by the end of the meeting), while Britain had won just six gold medals. Despite this, one preview prior to the Marathon believed that 'we will have the first six men home'.[41]

The Olympic Marathon began in the grounds of Windsor Castle and at the start the athletes were lined up in four rows, with Jack Price placed in the second row, accompanied by fellow Brit, Fred Appleby.[42] From the off, Price positioned himself towards the front of the field, along with several other British athletes; most notably Thomas Jack, who lead the field almost from the off, but after reaching five miles in just 27 minutes he dropped down to a walking pace and out of the race.

On a day described as 'Tropical'[43] in one newspaper report, Price, alongside fellow British athletes Fred Lord and Alexander Duncan and

---

[38] W.W. Alexander, 'Athletic Notes', *Sporting Mail*, 7 November 1908, 1.

[39] 'The Olympic Games: The Marathon Race', *The Times*, 25 July 1908, 8.

[40] Jose Harris, *Private lives, public spirit: Britain 1870-1914*, (Abington: Oxford University Press, 1993), 242; David Andrews, 'Sport and the Masculine hegemony of the modern nation: Welsh rugby, culture and society, 1890-1914' in John Nauright and Timothy Chandler, *Making Men: Rugby and masculine identity*, (London: Routledge, 1996), 55.

[41] W. W. Alexander, 'Athletic Notes', *Sporting Mail*, 18 July 1908, 1.

[42] Bryant, *26.2: The incredible true story*, 213.

[43] 'The Olympic Games', *Birmingham Daily Mail*, 25 July 1908, 4.

the South African Charles Hefferon, made up the lead group after Jack dropped out. In his analysis of the race, historian John Bryant describes that these men had been 'sucked' into what was a 'suicidal pace'. [44]

After thirteen miles, Price was in the lead alone, reaching the distance in 1:15:13, 13 seconds ahead of Hefferon. Price's own race would be over at 17½ miles, as Bryant describes, 'while still in the lead, Price staggered to the side and sat down'. Fred Hatton wrote in the *Athletic News*, 'A sudden collapse, the terrific heat of the sun, an equally strong pace, were all joining forces that betokened the early retirement of the Birmingham man; spent by his own folly and lack of forethought'.[45] This was to be the end of Price's Olympic marathon.

The comments from the *Athletic News* were certainly echoed by Price himself. For this he blamed the British officials who had advised him prior to the race. As part of a series of articles he wrote for Birchfield Harriers magazine *The Stagbearer* from 1932, he remarked:

> Disappointing to me, not because I failed, but because a great event like an Olympic Marathon was won in 2 hours 56 mins. whereas a few weeks previously I had run very nearly the same distance over a harder course in 2 hours 37 mins.

> My belief is that there were four men running that day for Gt. Britain who were all capable of beating 2 hours 40 mins. Why they failed was purely lack of experience, for the Marathon at that time was a new distance for English athletes.

> If there was one man that day who contributed more than others to the downfall of many competitors, then that man was Tom Longboat, of the Canadian team. Longboat was a great runner; he claimed a blood lineage of Indian, Irish and something else.

> He was brought to Ireland a few weeks before the Olympic Games to finish his training, and it was given out freely that Longboat could and would do 2 hours 30 mins for the race.

> Just before the race started, I was advised by two officials to hold Longboat if I could, their idea being that my stamina would beat him at the finish. Always a slow beginner, however, it was the worst advice they could have given me, as I realised too late.

---

[44] Bryant, *26.2: The incredible true story*, 215.
[45] Ibid, 216.

True, I held Longboat alright and paid the price. At 13 ½ miles Longboat cried enough and left me in the lead 400 yards in front of C. Hefferon (South Africa). But my task was hopeless, for the pace had been much too fast, and at 17 miles my legs refused to function and I gave up'.[46]

The indication from Price appears to be that his own inexperience and the universal in-experience of marathon running within the British team was at fault for the failure. As Price remarked and had demonstrated throughout his career, he was a self-proclaimed 'slow beginner',[47] and he relied on a strong finish to bring him his success. Leading from the front and at such a pace on a hot day were not the tactics he was accustomed to, nor would attempt once again in his career.

Price was certainly not the only British runner to suffer this fate. Out of the eleven British athletes that began the race, only four finished. The first British athlete home was Billy Clarke in twelfth position and nearly 21 minutes behind gold medallist, Johnny Hayes. The result represented a disaster for the British and in the aftermath of the marathon, the British press were critical about their athletes' approach. An *Athletic News* editorial was particularly damning:

> The plan of each British runner seemed to be, 'The devil take the hindmost'. Their very keenness to take the lead proved the reason of their downfall. It is all the same old story of the observance of old-fashioned theories. Had a team manager of experience been appointed even a fortnight before to look after the British Marathon men had good advice and good attendance been vouchsafed the men, matters might have been different. But I do think the chance of a marathon victory was absolutely washed.[48]

The first part of this quote certainly is relevant to Price, whose own 'keenness' ensured that he failed to run his own race. Price does mention being given advice by 'two officials', although there is no indication as to who they were and in what capacity they were giving advice. The *Sporting Life* was equally as frustrated, remarking, 'the failure was due to lack of judgement and proper preparation rather than to the heat of the day or any other cause'.[49] Whereas, the *Birmingham Daily Mail* believed that Britain, the self-proclaimed 'home' of distance running

---

[46] Jack Price, 'My Marathon Experiences', *The Stagbearer* 8. Vol 1, (November 1932), 3.

[47] Ibid.

[48] 'The Marathon failure', *Athletic News*, 27 July 1908, 1.

[49] 'The Olympic Games: A critical review', *Sporting Life*, 28 July 1908, 7.

was 'not altogether pleased to be forced to realise that in this particular department of athletics we have apparently lost ground'. [50] The marathon race proved once again that in track and field athletics the United States was superior to Britain, further damaging British pride.

Fig. 3. A permanent reminder: Jack Price Way. This leads to the Manor Abbey Stadium, the home of Halesowen Athletic and Cycling Club.

Conclusions

Jack Price, like all of his compatriots, failed in his attempt to win the 1908 Olympic marathon. The decision to be at the front of the race from the start appears to have been fatal to his chances. Undoubtedly, Price would have been better served by relying on a strong finish, which had previously served him well and would continue to do so throughout his career.

In the following months, British distance runners, including Jack Price, became more experienced at running the Marathon, as in the aftermath of the Olympic Marathon the event underwent its own brief 'boom' in Britain. One of the first marathon's organized in the wake of the Olympics took place in Bristol on 31 October 1908 over a distance of 23 miles (many of the marathons which were organized fell short of the now accepted length 26 miles 385 yards but were still considered as marathons). Price was victorious in this race, and as he noted in 1932,

---

[50] 'The Olympic Games', *Birmingham Daily Mail,* 25 July 1908, 2.

this came about through the use of tactics much more familiar to him than had been applied in the Olympic marathon:

> Having learned my lesson and deciding to leave the leaders alone during the early part of the race, at half distance I was not in the first dozen and nearly five minutes behind the leaders, Barrett, Beale (Polytechnic) and Lord (Wisbey Park). The latter was a very consistent yet unfortunate performer in Marathon races, for he was placed in about six races without winning one. Alas, poor Fred has passed on and with him a real sportsman.

> When entering Bristol Rovers' Ground, I was on the heels of F. Lord, with a mile still to do, and I won by nearly a lap.[51]

In 1909, marathons began to appear across the country and Price enjoyed great success in these races, winning on four occasions during that year in Cheltenham, Pontypridd, Malvern and Peterborough. In the Autumn of 1909, Price turned to a different challenge; the 25-mile track record which he had come so close to during the Birmingham marathon trial. On two separate occasions at Stourbridge and latterly at Kidderminster, Price was to come close on both occasions, but ultimately, he was to fail to break G.A. Dunning's record.[52]

In December 1909, Price turned professional. He described his reasoning for this decision as; 'at that time I was employed, as I am to-day, by Messrs. Stewart and Lloyd's, and things being quiet, I decided to try and improve my position by winning the Powderhall race, which at this time was one of the greatest annual events.'[53] The Powderhall marathon, held in Edinburgh on 3 January 1910, itself was a by-product of the marathon boom, having being held for the first time the previous year. In this race, Price trailed coming into the final mile but left his nearest opponent 'standing'[54] in the final yards to win 2 hours 40 minutes and 7½ seconds, receiving £75 and a gold watch. Following this, Price established himself as one of the leading professional distance runners

[51] Jack Price, 'My Marathon Experiences', *The Stagbearer*, November 1932, No 8. Vol 1, 3.

[52] 'Price v Record: Small Heath Harrier runs well at Stourbridge', *Sports Argus*, 18 September 1909, 8; W.W. Alexander, 'Athletic Notes', *Sporting Mail*, 16 October 1909, 1.

[53] Jack Price, 'My Marathon Experiences', *The Stagbearer* No. 8. Vol 1 (November 1932) 5.

[54] 'Pedestrianism: Powderhall Marathon', *Sporting Life*, 4 January 1910, 2.

in Britain, competing in numerous races over varying distances against multiple and single opponents for financial reward.

In 1914, Price joined the British Army and was placed in the Royal Artillery Regiment. Little is known of his activities during the war, although he did write letters to A.E. Machin who wrote for Birmingham sporting periodical *Sport and Play and Wheel Life* and remarked in April 1917 that he had met the man he had set out to 'keep hold of' during the Olympic Marathon', the Canadian Tom Longboat.[55]

After being demobilised from the Army on 2 February 1919, Price briefly returned to the amateur ranks, competing in the 1919 Polytechnic Marathon where he represented his regiment, finishing sixth. [56] Following this, Price competed in professional contests once again, before founding Halesowen Athletic and Cycling Club in 1923.

---

[55] A.E. Machin, 'Athletic Notes: Further News of Jack Price', *Sport and Play and Wheel Life*, 28 April 1917, 8.
[56] 'The Marathon Race', *The Polytechnic Magazine*, July 1919, 82.

6

Otto Herschmann: A Biographical Reassessment

Gherardo Bonini

Abstract

Winner of two Olympic medals in 1896 (swimming) and 1912 (fencing), and a later victim of Holocaust in 1942, Otto Herschmann must be re-evaluated as innovator of Austrian sport. A former Orthodox Jew, then assimilated as a sincere patriot, following his Olympic experience in 1896 he co-founded WAC a multi-tasking club modernizing Austrian athletics, introducing jumping, throwing and a modern training culture. Herschmann led his club to separate modern fencing from armoury, and after World War I his diplomacy brought prestige to Austria. A brilliant publicist and author of an under-rated book in 1904, from 1911 to 1914 he acted as President of Austrian sport trying to renovate national sport, he succeeded in bringing US coach Copland to manage Austrian athletics for a while. Dismissed in 1916 from the swimming federation's Presidency, he recovered after the War and enhanced his personal prestige as fencer, albeit being over forty.

Keywords: Modernization, Patriotism, Olympic Fencing, Reform, Herschmann.

Introduction

The most reliable Austrian and international sources on Otto Herschmann limit themselves to a summary of the most important steps in his career as both athlete and trainer, underlining above all his two Olympic medals, won 16 years apart and in two separate sporting disciplines. The second medal he won when he was President of the Olympic Committee for Austria, his country of origin. Another important moment in his life was when he wrote *Viennese Sport*, a book which was grossly underrated when published, and considered a mere presentation of the sporting situation in Austria, although later it was interpreted as a profound sociological and cultural expression of Austria at the time. Furthermore, Herschmann was one of the unfortunate victims of the Holocaust, which finally gave him the recognition he deserved for his sacrifice.[1]

A fact which requires greater clarification, is that the more specialist sources never dated in precise temporal terms his contributions to the spheres of swimming and fencing.[2] This study, even if purely based on secondary sources and a meticulous analysis of the journalistic articles of the day, has however reconstructed a figure deserving of greater attention, an innovator in Austrian sporting tradition. Some would say he was ahead of his time in both the social and cultural sense, moreover that he was more esteemed abroad than in his home country.

In the immediate post-War period, against the backdrop of a radically changed social-cultural environment, Herschmann finally earned, as a trainer rather than as an athlete, the recognition that had been denied to him during the war years. This analysis highlights how the common denominator in all Herschmann's activities was the reaction towards modernity in the implementation of a project that consisted in the complete renovation of Austrian sport, having at his disposition, albeit for a brief period, the efficient tools necessary for restructuring. In future, it will be necessary to explore the dynamics of this with more appropriate archival sources.[3]

[1] A short profile in (editor) Joseph Siegman, *Jewish Sports Legends. International Jewish Hall of Fame*, (New York: International Jewish Hall of Fame, 2005), 59. For *Wiener Sport* in Alexander Juraske, ,Die Jüdische Sportbewegung im Wien der Zwischenkriegszeit', in (editors) Bernahard Hachleitner, Matthias Marschik, Georg Spitaler, *Sportfunktionäre un Jüdische Differenz. Zwischen Anerkennung und Antisemitismus. Wien 1918 bis 1938.* (Berlin Germany and Boston MA : De Gruyter Oldenbourg, 2019), 71-74. On Herschmann as fencer, Michael Wenusch, *Geschichte des Wiener Fechtsports im 19. Und 20. Jahrhundert*, (Vienna : WUV, 1996), 88-90 and 348-352. On Herschmann as writer, Ralf Thies, *Wiener Großstadt-Dokumente, Erkundungen in der Metropole der k.u.k. Monarchie*, (Berlin, Forschungsschwerpunkts Technik Arbeit Umwelt am Wissenschaftszentrum Berlin für Sozialforschung, 2001), FSII =1 503, 3-47.
[2] Wrong data in 'Österreich Sportland' in (editor) Carl Kosik, *Österreich 1918-1934*, (Vienna : Heimattreue Volkschriften, 1935), 403, and in Norbert Adam, *Schwimmania*, (Vienna : Verband Österreichische Schwimmvereine, 1999), 10.
[3] Archives of Austrian Olympic Committee are lacunose according Erwin Niedermann, *Olympische Bewegung in Österreich*, (Vienna: Edwin Bauer & Co, 1995), 93.

Athlete and Sporting Director for change

Born on 4 January 1877 in the Viennese district of Simmering into a wealthy Jewish family, Herschmann was enrolled as a young man in the Viennese Technical Institute, where he began to swim within the ranks of the renowned association, *Erste Wiener Amateur Schwimmclub* (*First Vienna swimming club*), better known by its acronym EWASC. The name Herschmann began to appear regularly in the sporting press from the summer of 1893. He demonstrated an impressive capacity to master new skills, learning diving techniques and the basics of water polo.[4] In 1895, the year he registered at University in the faculty of law, he also made a decisive choice by notifying the Community for Jewish Worship in Vienna of his decision to leave the Orthodox religion.[5]

In 1896, Herschmann faced a crucial turning point. At the beginning of the year, the book by Theodor Herzl, *Die Judenstaat* (*The Jewish State*) was published and was met with disgruntlement by members of the EWASC, who reacted by forbidding access to the club by Jewish swimmers. However, they did not go so far as to insert the Aryan paragraph in its statutes.[6] Even though Herschmann was not one of the best Viennese swimmers,[7] due to the state of unpreparedness of the Austrian team in relation to the new-look Olympics, he was selected to compete along with his fellow club member Paul Neumann, also a former orthodox Jew, who won the 500 metres freestyle at Athens. Herschmann came in second in the 100 metres freestyle after the Hungarian, Alfred Hajos, even if his placing was not officially recognized until 2012.[8]

At the Athens Games, the swimming competitions had none of the great British swimming champions contending such as Jack Tyers and John Henry Derbyshire, nor the star German swimmers.[9] On his return to

---

[4] *Allgemeine Sport Zeitung*, July 23, 1893, 775, also August 12, 1894, 912.

[5] Anna Staudacher, '....*meldet den Austritt aus dem mosaischen Glauben*'. *18.000 Austritte aus dem Judentum in Wien 1868-1914. Namen, Quellen, Daten*, (Zürich : Peter Lang, 2009), 245.

[6] Bernhard Hachleitener, 'Arierparagraphen und anderen Ausschussmechanismen' in (editors) Hachleitner, Marschik, Spitaler, *Sportfunktionäre*, 35.

[7] In the unofficial European championships of Vienna in 1895 in the mile, Herschmann placed 5th only, *Sportvilàg* (Budapest), August 11, 1895, 6.

[8] In his writing in *Allgemeine Sport Zeitung*, April 26, 1896, 402, Herschmann confirmed his 2nd place. On 24 July 2012, Austrian journal *Kurier* reports the officialization in https://kurier.at/sport/nach-116-jahren-silber-fuer-otto-herschmann/805.357 (accessed October 20, 2018).

[9] Tyers dominated English and international swimming from middle to long distances. Derbyshire was the best specialist of 100 yards.

competition in the Imperial pools, Herschmann had the same ranking he held prior to Athens, confirming that he had benefited on the Olympic stage of favourable circumstances, which had boosted his chances. His post-Olympic efforts were mainly aimed at overhauling the sporting culture of his country. He wrote reports for the famous newspaper *Allgemeine Sport Zeitung* (*All Sports Journal*) and *Fremdenblatt* (*Foreigner Mail*), which had a more liberal outlook.[10]

Herschmann was greatly impressed by the performances of US champions in athletics, a discipline that did not exist in Vienna but existed instead in Prague and Budapest. Two days after his return to Vienna, along with some fellow club members, Herschmann arrived at a town square in Prater and timed a spontaneous race of 500 metres.[11] Herschmann recorded in writing his impressions of the Olympics which had been reported on by other experts, but his analysis proved the most convincing.

Austria had the potential to renew herself because she had the resources to do so, above all human resources, to be able to compete at the same level as the most illustrious nations. However, to do this, sporting activities would have to be overhauled. This could be done by promoting athletics such as running, high and low jumps and throwing sports, introducing intensive and continuous training sessions, giving assistance to athletes, introducing sporting activities in schools, presenting physical education to the youth, and as a result change the culture and approach to sport in a decidedly conservative country.[12]

Herschmann was motivated by a sincere sense of patriotism, although he battled with the delicate question of the nationalities, which animated and perturbed the Empire. To do justice to Austria, young and fresh talent from the bourgeois classes, the self-employed and university students would be required. There would need to be a confrontation between the indolent tendencies of the middle class, inserted into the Austrian administration and formed from lesser noble families and bureaucrats, who manifested little interest in athletic pursuits, contrary to their counterparts in Prague and Budapest.

---

[10] *Neues Wiener Tagblatt*, May 30, 1896, 30 and *Allgemeine Sport Zeitung*, July 26, 1896, 829.

[11] *Sport Tagblatt* mentioned the anecdote on September 11, 1936.

[12] 'Die Österreicher in Olympia' (The Austrian at Olympics), *Allgemeine Sport Zeitung*, April 26, 1896, 402. His collaborations with *Fremdenblatt* started in 1896, according to Thies, *Wiener Großstadt-Dokumente*, 31.

Along with other swimmers, he left EWASC and founded *Wiener Athletiksport Club* (WAC – *Viennese club for athletic sports*), the first Austrian sporting association with a multi-sport statute. In 1883, *Wiener Cyclisten Club* (*Viennese club for Cyclists*),[13] was founded and over the years the club created other sections, but only because it was encouraged to do so by its members. WAC, which was inspired along the Anglo-Saxon model, created sections for swimming, athletics, wrestling, fencing, soccer and field hockey.[14]

The sporting pages of *Neues Wiener Tagblatt* (*Daily for Viennese News*) of 22 September 1896 included a detailed article on the foundation of WAC, a sort of Club Manifesto, which gave the reader the sensation that the beginning of new era in Austrian sport was unfolding. The article was directed towards young Austrians, indicating very clearly the need for a physical and cultural regeneration. In this respect, it resounded with the position already taken by physiologists and educators in other European countries.[15] The clubs would be equipped with adequate medical facilities and the best trainers would be hired. The 'manifesto' was not solely Herschmann's idea but, without a doubt, his global alignment to it was the result of his own Olympic experience and his belief that an increase in sporting quality would coincide with an increased cultural awareness of health in general. Herschmann continued to make similar appeals incorporating the same concepts and in particular he focussed his attention on the introduction of physical education in schools. Having as their target these ambitious objectives, WAC requested from its member higher ubscriptions so as to get the funding for the necessary facilities, transfers and training sessions.[16]

In 1898, thanks to its merger with *Viennese Lawn Tennis Club*, WAC inaugurated a tennis section, with the first women affiliates. In the same year, the club was in a strong enough position to organize major

---

[13] Merging with *Wiener Sportvereinigung* (*Viennese Association for Sport*) the *Wiener Cyclisten Club* in 1907 set up another multi-tasking club, the *Wiener Sportklub*.

[14] WAC, *1896-1946. Wiener Athletiksport Club*, (Vienna : 1946), 2.

[15] For Italy, Angelo Mosso put the model of English sports, as mentioned by Susanna Spezia, 'Emilio Baumann, Angelo Mosso e una famosa polemica', in (editors) Adolfo Noto, Lauro Rossi, *Coroginnica. Saggi sulla ginnastica, lo sport e la cultura del corpo*, (Roma : La Meridiana, 1992), 110. In Germany and in France, the renewal assumed a profile of hygienic, aesthetic and muscular regeneration, as mentioned by Alan Radley, *The Illustrated History of Physical Culture. Volume 1. The Muscular Ideal*, (London, Snapes & Preston, 2001), 46 and ssgg.

[16] Wenusch, *Geschichte des Wiener Fechtsports*, 89.

national and international competitions to mark the Jubilee of the Emperor's reign.[17]

In the four years leading up to the second edition of the Olympics in Paris in 1900, Herschmann was no longer considered part of the elite swimming category. Instead. he was a diving instructor and dabbled in water polo. At the same time, he was sporadically involved with wrestling and athletics, in particular the most technical of the athletic disciplines, pole-vaulting. Within the organizational structure of WAC, a pair of English university coaches, Blaky and Graimley, were responsible for athletics.[18]

While he was not one of the top officials of WAC, Herschmann was heavily involved in the negotiations for the constitution of the Austrian swimming federation in 1899 and of an athletic commission in 1900[19] which meant that WAC was in a position to send three representatives in athletics to Paris.[20]

In the four-year period up to the controversial Saint Louis Olympic Games of 1904, Herschmann won his only national title in 1903 with the WAC water-polo team,[21] but first and foremost he was concentrating on achieving a certain level in fencing, under the direction of the famous instructor Master Franceschini, employed by the club since 1897.[22]

A patriotic ideal of sporting glory
In 1904, within the framework of a big editorial project designed to valorise the great city of Vienna, Herschmann wrote *Wiener Sport* (*Viennese Sport*), a book that illustrated the sporting situation in the capital and indicated how success could be achieved. What is significant is that Herschmann was chosen to write the book, as such a work had traditionally been carried out for the previous twenty years by Victor

---

[17] The most important event took place on 31 July and 1 August with the European Championship for Greco-Roman wrestling coupled with the World championship of weightlifting. Regarding athletics, WAC organized the Austrian championship of 1000 metres and Viennese championships for 100 yards.

[18] In the pole vault, Herschmann exceeded 2,65, see *Neues Wiener Tagblatt*, October 2, 1899. The mention of the two English athletes and trainers in *Neues Wiener Tagblatt*, December 3, 1896.

[19] *Allgemeine Sport Zeitung*, February 19, 1899, 187 and June 7, 1900, 1114.

[20] They were Hermann Wraschtil, Carl Lubowiecki e Siegfried Flesch, see Bill Mallon, *The 1900 Olympic Games, Results for All Competitors in All Events, with Commentary*, (Jefferson, North Carolina: McFarland & Company, 1998), 259-260

[21] WAC, *25 Jahre.*, Vienna, 1921, 12.

[22] About Franceschini, Wenusch, *Geschichte der Wiener Fechtsports*, 88.

Silberer, who was the owner of the influential *Allgemeine Sport Zeitung* (*All Sports Journal*), which had been publishing since 1880 and which had dealt with the diverse sporting disciplines up until now. Silberer was President of the Rowing Federation and was involved in all developments in the sport in Austria. He enjoyed cordial relations with journalists and the privileged Viennese social classes of the period.[23]

In his book, Herschmann categorizes sports according to their social roots, aristocratic, bourgeois and working class, then by type, dedicating specific chapters to weightlifting and wrestling, swimming and canoeing, fencing, winter sports (ice-skating, tobogganing and skiing), soccer, motorsports, and finishing the book off with a review of international competitions, interpolating the analytic sections with a specific chapter on Jews in sport.

The work sought to promote the creation of a sporting community that could disseminate a new and modern mentality, a stimulating role model for a wider social renewal. Herschmann said that the state must begin to devise a policy for sports and begin to liaise with its representatives if they really wanted tangible progress. Hungary and the Bohemia were active and were represented in the International Olympic Committee (IOC), while Austria is absent.[24]

A clear methodology was required. Herschmann speaks of Austria but does not explicitly use the geo-political term of Cisleithania, effectively Austria which includes the Bohemia, and which was not limited to the single German entity of its political territory. The presence of Bohemia in the IOC led to the perception of Austria as opposed to Cisleithania.

Herschmann explained in depth his sincere 'Cisleithanian' patriotism, with all the national components of the state, reasserting concepts already expressed in his previous articles. He clearly stated that Austria enjoyed international credibility in weightlifting and in figure skating, but it also had the potential to emerge in other disciplines that received little state attention and no training within the school system.

He indicated some encouraging phenomena that necessitated support so they could take off at a national level; the main results were in fencing, particularly in Vienna, with the Zdarsky School in skiing, and

23 About Victor Silberer, see Rudolf Müllner, 'Sport and Media.Austria before 1900' in (editors) Arnd Krüger and Wolfgang Büss, *Transformationen, Kontinuitäten und Veränderung in der Sportgeschichte*, (Hoya : 1988), Volume I, 87-90.
24 Otto Herschmann, *Wiener Sport*, (Vienna : 1904), 8-10.

in swimming, which would be seen in competitions where Austrian swimmers were on par with their Hungarian rivals and only slightly behind the British champions.[25]

As mentioned before, Herschmann dedicated an important chapter of his book to Jews in sport. He, himself, had decided to distance himself from his Jewish faith by assimilation, which, at the time, was a patriotic choice for him. To defend the colours of his Austrian (Cisleithanian) motherland smoothed out any internal conflicts he might have had. The Zionist position risked damaging Jewish athletes by inciting the latent anti-Semitism of the Aryans.[26]

Bourgeois fencing

In September 1904, Silberer wrote an article for *Allgemeine Sport Zeitung*, in which he sounded the alarm on the backwardness of Austrian sport, underlining how the presence of Jiri Guth Jarkovsky within the IOC was a bonus for Bohemian interests but not for Austria (Cisleithania).[27] Ahead of the preparations to organize an Austrian team for the Athens Olympic Games in April 1906, Hershmann and Siberer shared the same objectives. Moreover, Silberer's son (Herbert), a renowned enthusiast for aerial sports, was involved in fencing in WAC.[28]

The position of Herschmann was unique, a manager but also an accomplished fencer in his own right, and by opening a fencing section, WAC was effectively bringing Viennese fencing to Olympic standard. This marked a change with the past where it was

---

[25] Herschmann, *Wiener Sport*, 75.

[26] Herschmann, *Wiener Sport*, 25-27. Good comments in Alexander Juraske, *Die Jüdische Sportbewegung im Wien*, 71-73.

[27] *Allgemeine Sport Zeitung*, October 2, 1904, 1203. Cisleithania was geo-political name for Austria and entered into force after the *Ausgleich* (Compromise) of 1867 that gave birth to the Austro-Hungarian Empire. Cisleithania comprised Bohemia. Stephan Vajda, *Storia dell'Austria. Mille anni fra Est e Ovest*, (Milano : Bompiani, 1980), 419.

[28] The best article by Herbert Silberer *Die Erste Fahrt der Aero-Klub* (*The first Journey of Aero Club*) in *Allgemeine Sport Zeitung*, August 18, 1901, 947. He placed fifth in foil in the Jubilee Tournament 1908.

considered an almost aristocratic reserve, imbued with rituals, specialized academies and select tournaments, where the competitive result was of little real importance. Fencing in the armoury was not hostile to duels but was opposed to fencing as an Olympic sport; classificatory, athletic and competitive. The organizational chart of WAC with Count Thurn von Valassina at its head, accepted and welcomed this tradition, but within an unequivocal sporting context.[29]

Only for the purpose of finding space for the Olympic Games within the Universal Exhibition in Paris in 1900 and Saint Louis in 1904, did the Olympics host tournaments for professional Masters, as it did in the unofficial games of Athens in 1906, so fencing remained exclusively for amateurs, managed by the Olympic movement.[30] At that time, an international governing body the *Union internationale d'escrime* (*International Union of Fencing*), controlled by 'Masters', was founded and the *Akademie der Fechtkunst* (*Academy of Fencing Art*, hereinafter *Akademie*) represented Austria. The *Akademie* was created on the 22 September 1904 by Luigi Barbasetti, the shining light of Viennese fencing from the outset when he almost single-handedly elevated the level of the sport in Austria.[31]

The WAC fencing section was entrusted to Giovanni Franceschini, who had graduated in Rome and had been a pupil of Barbasetti. WAC opened the doors to a more democratic recruitment of fencers, anyone who wanted to attend lessons could register. Like Herschmann, WAC wanted to encourage individuals to show their athletic capabilities. Remaining true to its vocation of opening to a wider Austrian public, WAC had welcomed into its fold numerous fencers of Jewish origins, drawing some negative attention to the club in the traditionally anti-Semitist world of Viennese fencing.[32]

For these reasons, WAC and *Akademie* disagreed when it came to the creation of a Provisional committee for the unofficial Olympic Games of Athens 1906, which at the start only envisaged the participation of *Akademie*. As a first step, with Silberer's support, Herschmann acted as

---

[29] About the emancipation of the fencing sport from armoury, good comments in Cécile Ottogalli, Gérard Six, Thierry Terret, *Histoire de l'escrime. 1913-2013. Un siècle de la fédération internationale d'escrime*, (Paris : Atlantica, 2013), 9-18.

[30] Bill Mallon, Ian Buchanan, *The 1908 Olympic Games, Results for All Competitors in All Events, with Commentary*, (Jefferson, North Carolina : McFarland & Company, 2000), 137-47.

[31] About Luigi Barbasetti and the *Akademie der Fechtkunst* (*Academy of Fencing Art*), again Wenusch, *Geschichte der Wiener Fechtsports*, 80.

[32] Wenusch, *Geschichte der Wiener Fechtsports*, 353.

representative for track and field events, and within a short time he had inspired the creation of an autonomous fencing federation, open to the academies and presided over by Adolf Richling of the imperial armed forces fencing club. Herschmann took on the role of Vice-President.[33] At this point, the Provisional Committee recognized him as a member in the position of representative of the new federation, while keeping at the same time *Akademie* delegates.[34]

At the Athens games, Austria sent Herschmann and other two WAC fencers, Martin Harden, who had been champion for a disbanded Austrian-German federation, and Ernst Königsgarten.[35] Even though he was eliminated, due to his poor physical condition, in the Olympic sabre tournament, Herschmann achieved a great individual result, which notably increased his international prestige. In fact he was called up to become a jury member for four categories, i.e. athletics, wrestling and gymnastics, swimming and diving, fencing and football.[36]

Unfortunately, his international success counted for little in his home country where the fencing federation did not succeed in encouraging newcomers in other associations. More certain was the traditional pool for military and aristocratic recruitment, which the rival *Akademie* favoured as it was equipped with a technical commission to apply correctly the rules of its competitions. The *Akademie* also retained the trust of the amateur sections and organized the Austrian Championships for the 13-14 May 1906. In the sabre category, Herschmann was the only civilian to reach the finals, where he competed against five soldiers and came third.[37]

Apparently, the two federations were not in conflict. The *Akademie* organized Austrian championships where general registration was guaranteed. The bourgeois federation, which had instituted a genuine technical commission, tried sometimes to organize championships, but was forced to give up,[38] as they feared an almost certain boycott. The

---

[33] *Allgemeine Sport Zeitung*, March 4, 1906, 216.

[34] *Allgemeine Sport Zeitung*, February 18, 1906, 167.

[35] Bill Mallon, *The 1906 Olympic Games, Results for All Competitors in All Events, with Commentary*, (Jefferson, North Carolina : McFarland & Company, 1999), 175-177. The Austrian-German Federation was founded in 1897, but collapsed in 1901, see Deutsche Fechter Bund, *50 Jahre Deutsche Fechter Bund*, Berlin 1961, 11.

[36] Mallon, *The 1906 Olympic Games*, 37, 76, 79, 83, 99, 106, 127, 149.

[37] *Allgemeine Sport Zeitung*, May 20, 582.

[38] A stiff polemic rose against Viennese championship 1905 that announced by WAC, see *Allgemeine Sport Zeitung*, March 12, 1905.

public for modern events was not the same as the ritual gatherings offered in the academies offered by 'Masters' and military institutions. The presumption that there was a lack of appropriate education and that the civilian club did not inform their supporters on how to behave correctly, led to sharp criticism of them.[39]

Both the federations were impotent in the face of Austrian's failure to send a complete delegation to the London Olympic in 1908. Adequate funding was not provided for the 58 prospective participants,[40] so only seven were sent to London including representatives of the WAC.[41] In 1908, the most important sporting event in Austria was the Jubilee for the sixty years of Emperor Franz Joseph's reign. In this competition, Herschmann achieved a very satisfactory result, classified second place in the sabre tournament and fourth place in the foil tournament.[42] At the end of the year, the Olympic champion Jenö Fuchs visited Vienna seeking to meet Herschmann, who missed the Olympics for financial problems. In the bout, Fuchs was victorious, but Herschmann offered formidable resistance, confirming his status among the elite of the sport.[43]

The bourgeois federation could only organize a federal championship in the Spring of 1909, but in the same year it achieved general acclaim by organizing the University championships.[44] The students could participate in the academies, but they did not have an autonomous classification or an annual incentive. At that stage, *Akademie* and the federation inspired by Herschmann came to an agreement with the co-organizing of the national championships.[45]

Meanwhile, in the political field, the unresolved national conflicts and the deteriorating international situation created by the Austrian annexation of Bosnia imposed on the Austrian (Cisleithanian) State a greater cohesiveness since by this stage it was preparing for war.[46] In the sporting field, the political authorities pushed to impose a new national order, unified and cohesive, and, it understood the need for the creation of a permanent organ for the administration of national

---

[39] *Allgemeine Sport Zeitung*, April 5, 1908, 355.

[40] *Allgemeine Sport Zeitung*, March 1, 1908, 203-204.

[41] Mallon, Buchanan, *The 1908 Olympic Games,* 419.

[42] *Allgemeine Sport Zeitung*, June 28, 1908, 800-801.

[43] *Allgemeine Sport Zeitung*, October 31, 1908, 1371.

[44] *Allgemeine Sport Zeitung*, March 28, 1909, 342 and May 16, 1909, 588.

[45] *Allgemeine Sport Zeitung*, April 3, 1910, 353.

[46] Alexander May, *The Hapsburg Monarchy. 1867-1914*, (New York: Norton, 1968), 426-428.

sports.[47] At the head of this new 'Cisleithanian' body, to which all the federations referred back to, a personality was required that was motivated by sincere patriotism and familiar with the management of a modern sports federation. The experience of WAC had shown that it could function at a national level and, after a year as vice-President under the guidance of Hans Hornacsek, Otto Herschmann took on the role of President in December 1911.[48] The disintegration of the fencing federation headed by Herschmann and its merging with the *Akademie* demonstrated capability, a sense of compromise and sensibility to national interests towards Cisleithania. A sub-federation functioned within the *Akademie* to safeguard the interests of amateur athletes.[49]

Tasks and attempts at innovation

The immediate job of Herschmann at the head of this new federal body, the Central Commission for Sports, was to prepare for the Stockholm Games, where he himself won a silver medal in the sabre team, facilitated to some extent by the French boycott of the Games. Herschmann was the fourth athlete to win two medals in different disciplines, but this time he did not take advantage of the under qualified competition of the Athens Olympics.[50] In fencing, his was an authentic rise from zero to elite athlete.

The task in the mid-term of the official Central Commission was to prepare for the Olympics of 1916, planned for Berlin, and to prepare for the ranking of Austria among the top nations. In November 1913, Herschmann dedicated himself to the most difficult assignment of his mandate, visiting the USA in search of a national athletic trainer. During his trip, he expressed sincere admiration for the training facilities, the available resources and the organization of American sport, replicating that which he had always thought and wrote about.[51] On the question of resources, the prospect of substantial economic investment would have alarmed most probably the Austrian sporting and political circles. At home, Herschmann's trip passed almost unobserved and was

---

[47] *Allgemeine Sport Zeitung*, December 18, 1910, 1677.

[48] *Allgemeine Sport Zeitung*, December 17, 1911, 1713.

[49] Herschmann assumed ad hoc the Presidency and superseded the negotiations, *Neues Wiener Tagblatt*, May 6, 1911.

[50] Three athletes, i.e. the German Schumann (gymnastics/wrestling), Hofmann (athletics/gymnastics) and Australian Flack (athletics/lawn tennis) did double achievement in 1896.

[51] For instance, *Marion Star*, November 18, 1913.

focussed primarily on concrete results, i.e. recruitment of the renowned coach Bill Copland.[52]

Herschmann was not reappointed. Some of his projects, such as the construction of a new stadium in Vienna for track and field remained a dream.[53] Baron Colloredo Mansfeld, member of the IOC, succeeded Herschmann at the apex of Austrian sport. After Silberer's complaint concerning Bohemia's participation in the IOC in 1904, Austria succeeded in a process of marginalization of Bohemia in international sporting organizations, although there remained the original stronghold, the Bohemian presence in the IOC. Colloredo Mansfeld, who, as President of the Austrian Tennis Federation had succeeded in blocking the official entry of Bohemia in the relevant international federation, had the right profile to represent Austria at the IOC congress in Paris in June 1914, where Bohemia was officially expelled.[54]

Herschmann remained an important figure in Austrian sport and was appointed President of the Swimming Federation (VÖS), his original sport. Unfortunately, adding to his tasks as a lawyer in 1912 meant that he was not present in the major swimming events during the war. He had the misfortune in March 1916 to be given the responsibility of resolving a conflict between two clubs, *Freya* and EWASC, but he was not successful. As a result, he was substituted by Karl Kammerer and subsequently left the swimming federation.[55]

Post-War period: History concedes a rematch
Once the conflict was over, Herschmann was seen as an ex-athlete and ex-manager, someone who no longer counted, as he was not even a member of the steering committee of WAC anymore.[56] Since he was over 40 years of age, he decided that the only sport he could practice still was fencing and his comeback was so brilliant that he returned to the centre of attention in Austrian fencing circles. His victories while fencing for WAC between 1923 and 1924 gave him the title of best sabre man that Austria had ever produced. He brought the necessary quality

---

[52] *Allgemeine Sport Zeitung*, November 30, 1913, 1655.

[53] *Neues Wiener Sportblatt*, January 10, 1920, 2. The journal *New York Tribune*, December 3, 1913 estimated an expenditure of 800,000 US dollars.

[54] *Allgemeine Sport Zeitung*, February 22, 1914, 35. On the Bohemian expulsion from IOC, Gherardo Bonini, 'The Bohemian question in the international sporting organizations (1892-1914)', in (editors) Semmelweiss University Budapest, *6th Congress of ISHPES. Budapest, 14-19 July 1999. Proceedings*, (Budapest : Semmelweiss University, 2002), 340-341.

[55] *Neues Wiener Tagblatt*, May 20, 1916.

[56] *Neues Wiener Sportblatt*, January 20, 1920, III.

to the sport in competing against the best of the Hungarian fencers who dominated in the discipline.[57]

Despite being 47 years of age, the press wanted him to compete in the Paris Olympics,[58] but Herschmann knew his own limitations and did not participate but was content with becoming once again President of the jury for the Olympic selections. The *Akademie* was still at this point controlling Austrian sport and the amateur sub-federation.

In November 1924, Herschmann was internationally recognized. At the Paris Games a conflict broke out between the Italians and Hungarians, the 'Puliti case' so a return duel was organized between Puliti and Kovacs, which took place in Nagykanizsa, Hungary.[59] The two federations were unanimous in choosing Herschmann as President of the jury. In the reports on the duel, Herschmann was praised by both sides for stopping Kovacs at the right moment and persuading him to withdraw.[60]

In 1925, Austria was readmitted into the *International Fencing Federation* (FIE), which had been constituted in 1913. Herschmann was considered so highly abroad that it was impossible for him not to be appointed a representative for his country. He required however, an official position and *Akademie* offered him the Presidency of the amateur sub-federation,[61] to reward him for his patient diplomacy, as he had never been in irremediable conflict with *Akademie*.

Herschmann was appointed by the FIE as official referee and he always carried out the job with competence.[62] The FIE had begun a progressive separation of the activities of 'Masters' and in 1928 asked Austria to follow suit. In a changed social-economic context, with a bourgeois majority and a respected aristocracy, but nostalgically tolerated, the 1906 dream of Herschmann became a reality. The Austrian bourgeois sub-federation became the recognized authority for national fencing;[63] *Akademie* was relegated in the organizational chart and became

---

[57] The Italian journal *Gazzetta dello Sport*, March 19, 1924, 3 greeted the new spring of Austrian fencing.

[58] *Sport Tagblatt*, May 6, 1924.

[59] Thierry Terret, Jean Saint-Martin, Cecile Ottogalli-Mazzacavallo, 'The Puliti affair and the 1924 Paris Olympics : Geo-political issues, National pride and Fencing traditions', in *The International Journal of the History of Sport*, 25 (2007)10, 1381-1401. No mention for Herschmann's role.

[60] *Sport Hirlap*, November 13, 1924.

[61] *Sport Tagblatt*, February 17, 1925.

[62] *Escrime et tir*, 3(1926), 23.

[63] *Sport Tagblatt*, July 28, 1928.

responsible more specifically with armoury. Herschmann was appointed first federal President in 1928, even if with a provisional mandate. News of his appointment was revealed by Richard Brünner, who like Herschmann was an excellent fencer but also active in another sport, athletics.[64]

In 1928, Herschmann, after being awarded the Order of the Crown of the Kingdom of Italy, was honoured to be appointed Head Coach for sabre team for the Amsterdam Olympics.[65]

His patient diplomacy resulted in Vienna organizing the European Championship in 1931. In Vienna, Herschmann was not the President of the Organizing Committee, but was the real force behind the event, presiding over among other things, nearly all the Championship juries.[66] In one of these, he remained firm on a controversial decision, which lead to complaints and the withdrawal of the Italian fencers. The Hungarian press, who criticized in 1928 some of his decisions at Budapest in an Italian-Hungarian match, slyly insinuated that the Italian performances were not what they seemed and that they should not have been prize winners, applauded Herschmann. [67] Maybe he was just impartial on both occasions.

In 1932 at the Los Angeles Olympic Games, Austria finally won the first fencing title in its history with foilist Ellen Preis. The leading sporting paper in Austria, *Sport Tagblatt* (*Daily Sport Journal*) asked Herschmann and not Brünner to write an article on the significant win [68] and Herschmann reiterated the sport of fencing in Austria and its history. Preis had reached her objective thanks in part to the journey that Herschamann had undertaken. At this point Herschmann decided to step down from active participation in the sport.

He dedicated himself to his professional career as a lawyer. He did not abandon Austria after the Anschluss and he was affected by the Nazi decree of the 20 November 1938 forbidding all Jewish lawyers from

---

[64] Before World War I, Brünner won Viennese title for 100 metres in 1908. He won the Austrian foil title in 1920, 1924 and 1927, and in sabre in 1922, 1925

[65] *Sport Tagblatt*, July 20, 1928.

[66] Herschmann drove the press release, *Sport Tagblatt,* May 30, 1931. *Nemzeti Sport*, May 31, 1931 praised him for conduction of Jury.

[67] *Nemzeti Sport*, May 31, 1931.

[68] *Sport Tagblatt*, August 6, 1928.

practicing their profession.[69] He remained in Vienna until 18 February 1942, when he was deported to Sobibor, a secondary camp to Izbica, where he died somewhere between the 14 and 17 June 1942.[70]

Conclusions

Although he had chosen the road of assimilation rather than Zionism, Herschmann's roots were embedded in the Jewish culture, conserving a fundamental openness and enthusiasm towards progress and change, which clashed with the tendency to immobility and the perpetuation of the status quo by the Austrian bourgeois of the time. His choice of national identity derived from a strong element of 'Cisleithanian' patriotism, which was difficult to build on due to the contrasts between the nationalities. Herschmann contributed to diffusing the lessons of modernity, which he had himself learnt at the Athens Olympics, giving an inkling of a future development in Austrian sport, based on personal dedication, scientific training, and supported by the political administration with the base to be constructed in the schools. When he found the political and administrative means to act, he contributed significantly to the advancement of sport and culture in Vienna and Austria as a whole. Unfortunately, despite his diplomatic qualities and the prestige in which he was held abroad, he was ahead of his time, as he did not receive the necessary political, social and financial support for his ambitious project for a nationwide overhauling of Austrian sport.

---

[69] Barbara Sauer, Ilse Reiter-Zatloukal, *Advokaten 1938. Das Schicksal der in den Jahren 1938 bis 1945 verfolgten österreichischen ReichsanwältInnen und Rechtsanwälte*, (Vienna : Manz, 2010), 178.

[70] Siegman, *Jewish Sports Legends*, 159.

In the Interwar period, he was officially recognized for his efforts and had some success, particularly in the field of fencing, where he brought prestige to the sport in Austria.

He represented an important figure in Austrian sport and his name should be remembered alongside those other famous and celebrated assimilated Jews such as, Hugo Meisl, [71] coach of the famous *Wunderteam* (*Wonder Team*), and Theodor Schmidt,[72] President of the Austrian Olympic Committee from 1928 to 1937. Not by chance, they shared with Herschmann a refined sense of diplomacy, the same patriotic vision and the same desire to see Austria's prestige grow through sport and culture.

---

[71] About Meisl, Andreas Hafer, Wolfgang Hafer, *Hugo Meisl oder der Erfindung des modernen Fussballs. Eine Biographie*. (Göttingen : Verlag die Werkstatt, 2007)
[72] Matthias Marschik, *Theodor Schmidt. Eine Jüdische Apostel der Olympische Idee'*, (Berlin : Heinrich & Heinrich, 2018)

7

A Reality Check for the Barcelona 1992 Olympic Games

Carlos Garcia

Abstract

Over the years, the Barcelona 1992 Olympic Games have simultaneously become a founding myth of Spanish democracy and Spanish sport and the paradigmatic example of an Olympics Games with a positive legacy. After almost thirty years since its celebration, the time may have come to analyse to what extent this myth corresponds to reality. To do this, we will first analyse the different levels in which it has operated: as an example of the economic modernization of the country; as evidence of the democratic consensus in Spain; as a success story of elite sports policy; and as an example of urban renewal. The subsequent critical analysis will try to make emerge those aspects that the myth omits or hides. It is not about denying the positive aspects of those games, but to help clarify the debates about the sustainability of the main sports mega-event on the planet.

Keywords: Olympic Games, Spain, Barcelona 1992, Sports Policy, Doping.

Introduction

The Barcelona 1992 Olympic Games constitute one of the most important moments in Spanish history. They are considered a milestone in the process of modernization and democratization initiated after the death of the dictator Francisco Franco, and, at the same time, a moment of widespread consensus and optimism in Spanish society. The organizational and sporting success of the Games has become a key feature in the country's official memory, and for many Spaniards the Barcelona Games were *the best Games in history* and they continue to be so today.

Although the rest of the world does not necessary share that impression, especially not those countries who have also organized other Olympic Games, there is a certain international consensus about the success of Barcelona's Olympic legacy.[1] Compared to the ruin that was for Greece

---

[1] For example, the opening phrase in the article about the 1992 Olympic Games of the Encyclopedia Britannica online version states: 'The 1992 Games were

resulting from the 2004 Olympic Games or the abandoned facilities of Rio 2016, everyone seems to agree that the proof that hosting the Olympic Games can have a long-term positive impact for a city and a country are precisely the Games of 1992. Moreover, the Barcelona Games were the first ones held without a political boycott since 1972 and were surrounded by the historical optimism brought by the fall of the Berlin Wall and the end of the Cold War.

In any case, these Games represented a huge boost in visibility and global awareness of the city and the country, with the consequent increased expansion of urban and cultural tourism - and not only sun and beach tourism - and allowed a transformation of Barcelona into the open, cosmopolitan, service leaning city glowing in the happy days of globalization. However, just as globalization is a notion in crisis after the rise of so-called populisms and the resurgence of trade wars, perhaps it is also a good time to take stock of the impact of Barcelona 92 on Spanish society and its role as a hinge between a backward and reactionary Spain and a modern and cosmopolitan Spain.

Barcelona 1992 Myth: The best Olympics ever!
Before putting into question the myth of the Olympic Games in Barcelona, we must be familiar with it. This myth is based on four great and interrelated successes: the organizational success, the political consensus over the Games, the sporting triumphs of the Spanish team, and the urban legacy for the city. The four converge on a fundamental appreciation of Spanish twentieth century politics: the secular lag in the modernizing process suffered by Spain since the XIX century was only overcome with the arrival of democracy in 1978.

Organizational success
The organization of the Barcelona 1992 Olympic Games was an undisputable success. Although for a long time there were doubts about whether the facilities would be built on time, the truth is that when the time came they were all ready.[2] The opening ceremony also took place smoothly, and there were no major problems with accommodation, nor with press services or infrastructures for athletes.

---

perhaps the most-successful modern Olympics'. 'Barcelona 1992 Olympic Games', *Encyclopaedia Britannica*, 2019.

[2] The climax of the construction issues were the water leaks at the inauguration of the Olympic Stadium at the World Athletic Coup on September 9, 1989. See for example M.A. Santos, 'La Ceremonia de La Confusión', *El Mundo Deportivo*, 9 September 1989.

The symbolic content of the opening ceremony – which has been analysed elsewhere[3] – turned out to be, above all, an intelligent way of overcoming the political antagonisms of the moment – especially the potential clash between the Spanish and the Catalonian nationalisms – by redefining a concept of *mediterraneanity* adapted to the incipient postmodernity.

The key element of the ceremony was the choice of the artistic direction, which was bestowed to the theatre group *La Fura Dels Baus*. It was a multidisciplinary company of great prestige among the artistic avant-garde for its multimedia installations, the quality of its artistic design and for involving the public in its representations, breaking with the so-called fourth wall. There was a clear intention to associate the country with the international artistic vanguard. A decision very similar to that of the official song of the Games: a duet between the Barcelona opera singer Montserrat Caballé and the leader of Queen and pop megastar Freddy Mercury. That is, a representative of high culture, perhaps the furthest image from the widely extended idea of Spain's *flamenco* and *tapas*, along with one of the most famous pop singers in the world, someone completely removed from any traditionalism. The discourse was clear: Spain was no longer a conservative, Catholic and backward country, but a young, liberal, creative and global democracy.

This discourse connected with a deep intellectual and political tradition that went back at least until the end of the nineteenth century. In 1898, Spain lost its last colonies, Cuba and the Philippines, unleashing a deep political and institutional crisis that had its reflection in the intellectual world. For many of the Spanish intellectuals and writers of the time the defeat showed the Spanish backwardness, compared to the rest of Western powers, produced by its intellectual isolation and the dominant presence of the Catholic Church in the political arena. The solution, proposed by the most reputable Spanish intellectual of the time, was Europe. For Ortega y Gasset, Spain was losing the train of modernization and had to open up to the European intellectual and scientific currents if it did not want to stay behind forever.[4]

The idea that Spain had not had a process of modernization comparable to that of the rest of European nations, and that this industrial, political and social backwardness was an anomaly in Europe that explained its

---

[3] Miquel De Moragas, 'La Cultura Mediterránea En Los Juegos Olímpicos de Barcelona' 92' (Barcelona, 1993).

[4] Jesús J. Sebastián Llorente, 'La Idea De Europa De Ortega Y Gasset', *Revista de Estudios Políticos* 83 (1994): 221–45.

internal problems, became the strongest narrative to explain the nineteenth and the twentieth centuries in Spain. [5] Hence, when democracy was restored after the death of Franco, the objective of the political elites was not only to recover democracy, but to recover it as a tool for pending modernization. Therefore, the greatest political success of those early years of democracy was the entry into the European Economic Community in 1986. No wonder that the main television satirical program of that time was titled 'Ya semos europeos', *'We are finally Europeans'.*[6]

Political consensus
The Barcelona 1992 Olympic Games had from its origin a political tension between competing political parties and administrations.[7] The Games were taking place in Barcelona, the capital of Catalonia, a historical region with its own identity and governed by Convergència i Unió (CiU), a Catalan nationalist alliance of conservatives and Christian Democrats with a charismatic leader, Jordi Pujol, who was developing a policy of national affirmation. On the national level, the Spanish Socialist Workers Party (PSOE) had governed Spain since 1982 with an absolute majority. Led by the political star of the time, Felipe González, they combined a social democratic accent on social policy – education and health system improvements – and a socio-liberal economic policy – market-friendly reforms, industrial reconversion and public companies privatizations – benefiting from a society yearning to break with the Franco regime. Finally, the Catalan branch of the PSOE, the Socialist Party of Catalonia (PSC) governed Barcelona, the mayor being another charismatic figure who swept the elections, Pascual Maragall.

The years leading up to Games were a constant tug of war between the three administrations to monopolize the political gains of the operation and to control the symbolic projection of the event according to their interests. Disputes over the Organizing Committee of Barcelona 92 (COOB) followed one after another, but always with exquisitely

---

[5] Carles Sirera Miralles, 'Neglecting the 19th Century: Democracy, the Consensus Trap and Modernization Theory in Spain', *History of the Human Sciences* 28, no. 3 (20 July 2015): 51–67.
[6] The show was created by the Catalonian comedy group *Els Joglars* and aired on Spanish public television on November 4th, 1989. See Rosana Torres, 'Albert Boadella Presentó Anoche Su 'Sarcástica' Serie', *El País*, 31 October 1989.
[7] John Hargreaves, *Freedom for Catalonia? Catalan Nationalism, Spanish Identity and the Barcelona Olympic Games* (Cambridge: Cambridge University Press, 2000).

democratic manners.[8] This, in a country whose biggest trauma had been a civil war and a subsequent forty years dictatorship, was a sign that the country had changed and that violence would never be resorted to again to solve political discrepancies, nor would its politicians get Spaniards into a war between brothers.

This democratic pact was, without a doubt, the aspect that the political, intellectual and journalistic elites were most proud of, reflecting the way in which democracy had been restored.[9] Once Franco was deceased, the process of democratic transition had been carried out under a fundamental motto, that of forgiveness, reconciliation and a focus on the future. The exiled republicans who had lost the war, and their political grandchildren like the PSOE or the Communist Party of Spain (PCE) renounced any revenge, while the old Falangist[10] politicians accepted the return of the democratic regime they had fought during the civil war. For this, the fundamental figure had been that of King Juan Carlos I. Appointed successor by Generalissimo himself with the confidence that he would lead a similar –i.e. authoritarian – reign, he transformed Franco's regime into a liberal democracy by successfully sponsoring its self-dissolution. It was the figure of the monarch who ensured the loyalty of the military and avoided a coup d'état, allowing the development of a liberal democratic regime similar to any existing in Western Europe, including the legalization of the communists, black beast of the military, and the fascists.

The *spirit of the Transition* was born, a spirit of concord and reconciliation that replicated the idea of economic modernization at the political level: Spain aspired to stop being a country of military coups, political instability and persecution of political opponents to reach European stability and progressiveness. Economic modernization, with the development of the Welfare State and the growth of the middle classes, and political modernization, with a parliamentary system and civil liberties, created a virtuous circle that enabled Spain to overcome its dark history.

---

[8] Joan Botella, 'Los Juegos Políticos. Actores y Estrategias En Torno a Los Juegos Olímpicos de Barcelona 1992', in *Las Claves Del Éxito1*, ed. Miquel de Moragas and Miquel Botella (Barcelona: Universidad Autónoma de Barcelona, 1996), 177–87.

[9] For an overview of the democratic transition, see for example Javier Tusell, *La Transición a La Democracia (España, 1975-1982)* (Madrid: Espasa-Calpe, 2007); Álvaro Soto Carmona, *Transición y Cambio En España: 1975-1996* (Madrid: Alianza Editorial, 2005).

[10] Falange was the dictatorship's official party and the only one legal during that time.

The monarchy played a critical role in this evolution. The civil war had been unleashed by a military coup against the Second Spanish Republic (1931-1939), so the restoration of democracy could have been in the form of a republic. Many social strata lacked any confidence on the new monarch due to his collusion with the regime and Franco himself. However, Juan Carlos I not only promoted democracy, but also in 1981, he was decisive in stopping a reactionary military coup by taking the side of democracy and legality. His legitimacy was, therefore, beyond doubt both in the conservative camp and among the left. His son and successor, Prince Felipe, could not adduce in any way a service sheet like that of the father, so his legitimacy should come from other sources. In addition to being an exemplary student and child, he found in sport another way of legitimating his position. Thus, as an Olympian athlete – he competed in sailing – he was selected as the flagbearer of the Spanish delegation at the opening ceremony of the Games. In doing so, the prince was linking his non-elected status as future head of state with the meritocratic character of sport participation. In this way, sports meritocracy was projected on his figure: the prince would deserve the succession by showing that, despite not having been chosen for the position, he would be the best prepared to exercise it.

Sporting triumphs
Before the games, the Spanish athletes had won 26 medals since 1896: 5 gold, 12 silver and 9 bronze. In Barcelona'92, they won 22 medals, 13 gold, 7 silver and 2 bronze, almost equalling the joint results of one century of Spanish sport. Undoubtedly, the sporting success was key to reinforcing the idea of success of the Games.

In fact, Spain had already organized a major sporting event a few years before, the 1982 Soccer World Cup. As Simon Sanjurjo[11] has shown, despite a deep economic crisis, a political transition in process and almost daily terrorist activity,[12] the government managed to bring forward a World Cup with the added challenge of having seen an increase in the number of participating countries from sixteen to twenty-four during the build up to the event. However, the collective recollection of these championships is at best mixed or just plain sour, due to the Spanish national side's disappointing performance. Spain

[11] Juan Antonio Simón, 'El Mundial de Fútbol de 1982: Escaparate de La Nueva Democracia Española= The World Cup 1982: A Showcase of the Spain's New Democracy', *Materiales Para La Historia Del Deporte* 10 (2012): 87–104.
[12] In 1982 there were active the Basque separatist terrorist group *ETA*, the extreme-left terrorist group *GRAPO* and the government death-squads *Batallón Vasco-Español*.

played poorly and although it reached the second group stage, it did not reach the semi-finals creating a deep football crisis in a country where football was *el deporte rey* – the king of sports.

The government drew the appropriate lessons from that experience and implemented for the first time in history a plan to support and develop elite sport in Spain under the umbrella organization Asociación de Deportes Olímpicos (ADO).[13] New facilities were built, especially high performance centres - known as *Centros de Alto Rendimiento* (CAR) – and above all the ADO scholarships were created. These scholarships were a public-private collaboration by which the largest companies in the country sponsored an Olympic sport, and with this money, the federation awarded scholarships to the best-qualified athletes so that they could devote themselves to training during the entire four-year Olympic cycle. Thus, Spain got medals in some established disciplines in the country - like football - and in others in which there was hardly any tradition - like field hockey. In addition, not only did male athletes win medals, but also women athletes.

Until then, Spanish sport had lacked preparation, investment and results; athletes had failed in all major competitions; and the country suffered a deep delay in terms of popular practice rates. Finally, though, in the sporting arena the accelerated and triumphant modernization of the country could be asserted.

Barcelona's urban legacy
Last, but not least, there is Barcelona's urban and symbolic transformation into one of the main global cities of the world thanks to the Games, transforming its economy to successfully face the challenges of nascent globalization.[14]

From the beginning, the organizers clearly postulated that the Games should be an opportunity to transform and develop the city.[15] Spain, despite its successful democratic transition, did not enjoy a prosperous

---

[13] Manuel Llanos, 'Así Colaboró El Comité Olímpico Español En El Éxito Del 92', in *Las Claves Del Éxito*, ed. Miquel de Moragas and Miquel Botella (Barcelona: Universidad Autónoma de Barcelona, 1996), 68–87.

[14] Botella, 'Los Juegos Políticos. Actores y Estrategias En Torno a Los Juegos Olímpicos de Barcelona 1992'.

[15] Lluis Millet i Serra, 'Los Juegos de La Ciudad', in *Las Claves Del Éxito*, ed. Miquel de Moragas and Miquel Botella (Barcelona: Universidad Autónoma de Barcelona, 1996), 232–49.

decade during the eighties. The country suffered an accelerated process of deindustrialization and youth unemployment hit hard among the most vulnerable communities. The industrial nuclei of the country – Barcelona included – saw languishing strategic facilities such as commercial ports. One of the main transformations undertaken thanks to the Olympic impulse was that of the coastline of the city, dominated until then by the port and its industrial-related activities, which was transformed into a seafront. The city was opened to the sea and a decadent industrial hub was transformed into a potential tourist attraction.

Other urban transformations followed the same strategy. On the one hand, *finishing* the city by providing it with necessary infrastructures, and on the other, renovating the degraded downtown to make it appealing to tourists. The success of the model, supported by the international projection of the Games, was resounding, and Barcelona became a city at the forefront of the service economy and connected to the global economy, and at the same time one of the favourite tourist destinations in the world.[16]

At this point, we have finished our brief synthesis of what would constitute one of the best synergies produced by Olympism: national reconciliation and political consensus, cultural and economic transformation, sports success and national pride, and an effective urban transformation. It is logical, then, that even today a national consensus exists that places the Olympic Games of Barcelona 92 as the peak moment of the democratic period. It is time to ask, more than 25 years later, what remains of that success and to what extent it faithfully represents the Spanish reality then and now.

Barcelona 1992 reality check
After the financial crisis of 2009, the Euro crisis with its austerity policies and a decade of economic crisis and stagnation, high levels of unemployment and political instability, it is perhaps time to look back and analyse the Olympic Games again not to deny its success, which is hardly deniable, but to see to what extent that was a true reflection of Spain and its future or was actually a kind of mirage. For this, we will review the lessons of Barcelona 92 that we have just synthesized to carry out a reality check of each one of those successes.

---

[16] Pere Duran, 'Turisme: Els Impact Del Jocs i de La Seva Imatge Sobre El Turisme', in *Barcelona: L'herència Dels Jocs*, ed. Miquel de Moragas and Miquel Botella (Barcelona: Editorial Planeta, 2002), 275–94.

Spanish modernization derailed

Of all the achievements of Barcelona 92 undoubtedly the most significant and the one that seemed to change in depth the country's economic model and its cultural and ideological framework was the definitive, and forever longed for, modernization. What Spain had been trying for a century or so was to regain its place at the European consensus, and in 1992, we were finally Europeans. As we have said, it was a two-way Europeanization: economic Europeanization, after the failed industrialization of the nineteenth century, and political Europeanization, leaving behind crony capitalism and endemic corruption.[17]

As for the economic transformation, the first years after the Olympic Games saw strong economic growth, falling unemployment rates and economic internationalization thanks to the landing in Latin America of a group of newly created *national champions* formed out of former public monopolies. The robust economic growth meant that Spain surpassed Italy in nominal GDP and its Presidents requested their entry into the G7.[18] Unfortunately, the implosion of the financial crisis after the fall of Lehman Brothers in 2007 showed that in fact a large part of the Spanish miracle was based on an international credit bubble that had been fattening one of the biggest real estate bubbles in the world. The hangover left the country with one of the highest structural unemployment rates in Europe and an economy heavily dependent on external debt and tourism, a sector characterized by poor quality employment.[19]

As for the alleged Europeanization of political elites, the bursting of the housing bubble revealed a deep network of political corruption in which parties exchanged illegal donations in exchange for public contracts, at local, regional and national levels. At present, five former regional presidents have been accused of corruption, one has been already condemned and, in what is probably the most serious case of corruption of the democratic period, the conservative party, Popular

---

[17] Crony capitalism and corruption were widespread during both the Francoist dictatorship (1939-1975) and the monarchic period (1874-1931) where local political leaders controlled the elections through political patronage.

[18] Ana Carbajosa, 'España Supera Por Primera Vez a Italia En Riqueza Por Habitante', *El País*, 18 December 2007.

[19] Antonio Martín Sanabria and Bibiana García Medialdea, 'Lending Calling. Recession by over-Indebtedness: Description and Specific Features of the Spanish Case', *Panoeconomicus* 63, no. 2 (2016): 195–210, https://doi.org/10.2298/PAN1602195M.

Party (PP) has been condemned and its leaders accused of receiving systematic payments in exchange of public contracts, including ministers and possibly former Spain's prime minister, Mariano Rajoy.[20]

All this has considerably reduced the public's confidence in the degree of Europeanization of Spanish politics and economy, and the country now seems doomed to a perennially failed modernization. To make things harder, confidence in the European project in one of the most pro-European countries in the EU has been partially broken by the imposed austerity policies and by the realization that the Spanish credit bubble would not have been possible without the easy access to credit from the European bank system.[21] This resulted in a crisis of modernization and crisis of purpose, because the European horizon no longer seems the mobilizing project that was in the eighties, but an insensitive bureaucracy with deep democratic deficits.

Transición culture in crisis
Having lost any confidence in the Spanish economic miracle and among widespread political corruption, the only positive point remained the exemplary transition from dictatorship to democracy, a demonstration of forgiveness and reconciliation that, we were told, was studied in universities all over the world.

In fact, the transition was not as peaceful as it seemed - there were hundreds of deaths between 1975 and 1982 - and the reconciliation was possible only with some political price. The most critical being the absence of any avowal of responsibilities, whether criminal or symbolic, from the Francoist establishment who had led the murderous repression after their victory in the civil war and the subsequent victimization of political opponents for decades. There was no restorative justice whatsoever, and the Francoist political class was incorporated into democratic life without any act of contrition, along with the Francoist police and the judiciary, and of course the economic elites.[22]

---

[20] Fernando J. Pérez, 'Governing Popular Party and Its Ex-Treasurer, Sentenced in Massive Corruption Case', *El País*, 24 May 2018.
[21] In the last Eurobarometer, 69% of Spaniards thought Spain membership was a good thing generally speaking, but only 42% considered that their voice counted in the EU. See European Parliament, 'Spring Eurobarometer 2019. Closer To the Citizens, Closer To the Ballot' (Brussels, 2019).
[22] For a critical reprisal of *La Transición* see Juan Carlos Monedero, *La Transición Contada a Nuestro Padres* (Madrid: Catarata, 2017); Guillem Martínez, *CT o La Cultura de La Transición* (Barcelona: Debolsillo, 2012).

As a result, a narrow democratic consensus was built, in which many issues were left out, like the monarchy or the Catalonian referendum. An even more disturbing by-product was the absence of a clear rupture from Franco regime in the conservative Partido Popular (PP).[23] This passive acceptance of the dictatorship legacy may explain a Spanish anomaly: Partido Popular and liberal party Ciudadanos accepted the support of extreme-right party VOX in Andalucía region in April 2019 to form a government. It was the first time the extreme-right had any parliamentary representation in Spain and instead of supporting policies of non-cooperation with the extreme-right or taking years to whitewash and legitimize these formations, the Conservatives and the Liberals accepted their votes only a few weeks after their first electoral success. The agreements were replicated a few months later in tens of cities after the local elections.[24] The 'exemplary' Spanish democracy still has remnants of its past.

Doping and the Spaniards
The sporting success of the Spanish delegation is perhaps the most indisputable of all. Going from 26 medals in 100 years to 22 medals in a single edition of the Games is remarkable. The Spanish miracle was possible thanks to a lot of enthusiasm, the emotional advantage of competing at home, and vast resources made available for the first time to athletes up to then forgotten by public policies in a country which turned its back on everything that was not football. However, it is possible that the resources put at the disposal of Spanish sport were somewhat excessive.

The need for modernization of Spanish sport had been clearly identified by Spanish policy makers. In 1988, before the fall of the wall, the then president of the highest Spanish sports body, the Superior Council of Sports (CSD), Social Democrat Javier Gómez Navarro, had said that Spain needed laboratories such as those of the German Democratic Republic.[25] The ADO Plan actually bought a *biomedical unit* but we do not know what kind of material was acquired. We do know that one of the doctors in charge of the biomedical department was Nicolás

---

[23] The Partido Popular has refused several times to condemn Francoism, the last time in 2018. See Alejandro Torrús, 'PP y Ciudadanos No Se Suman a La Condena Del Franquismo Aprobada Por El Senado', *Público*, 21 November 2018.
[24] Sam Jones, 'Spanish Parties Enlist Support of Far-Right Vox to Control Madrid', *The Guardian*, 15 June 2019.
[25] Juan Mora, 'Gómez Navarro Quería Unos Laboratorios 'Tipo RDA'', *El País1*, 13 October 1988.

Terrados.[26] He continued his career as a sport physician at the cycling team ONCE in the nineties, including the 1998 Tour de France, under Manolo Saiz leadership, one of the cycling managers heavily involved in the Puerto affaire.[27]

Spain's commitment to elite sport coincided with the fall of communism in 1989 and some of the best coaches from other side of the iron curtain were hired by the Spanish government. Among those who arrived were the coaches of the Spanish Olympic cycling team, soviet Genari Gorounov and Alexandre Nizhegodtsev. Under their command, two cyclists tested positive during doping controls in that team. The first was José Manuel Moreno, future gold medallist in Barcelona '92, who was later cleared due to formal defects in testing.[28] The second, was the young and unknown Josep Taradellas, who not only denied the accusations, but decided to abandon cycling in the face of what he felt was an absence of explanations by the coaching staff and the doctors.[29] The press reported him saying 'I want to know what they have given me'.[30] The team denied the accusations, the federation supported the coaches and nobody heard anything about that athlete again. The doctor of that team had been Jesús Losa, accused years later of doping activities.[31] In 2019, a journalistic inquiry found proof of the Spanish Olympic cycling team hiring the doping celebrity Michelle Ferrari for the 1996 Atlanta Olympic Games.[32] Over the years, besides Nicolás Terrados, Doctor Sabino Padilla was accused of doping the footballer Carlos Gurpegui;[33] Luis García Del Moral and Pedro Celaya appeared in the USADA report over Lance Armstrong doping practices; and last but not least, Eufemiano Fuentes was the head of Operation Puerto,[34]

---

[26] 'ADO: Un Proyecto Único' (Madrid, 1993).

[27] José Lui Barbería, 'El Tour Castiga Al ONCE Con La Exclusión de Saiz y Del Médico Del Equipo', *El País*, 17 June 1999.

[28] 'La UCI Rehabilita a Moreno de Su Caso de 'Doping'', *El País*, 28 November 1991.

[29] 'Tarradellas, Del ADO, Abandona El Ciclismo Porque Dice Que Le Han 'Dopado'', *El País*, 27 November 1991.

[30] Robert Álvarez and Rafael Carbonell, 'El Presidente de La Federación Catalana Denuncia Cuatro Casos Más y La Existencia de Una Mano Negra', *El País*, 21 September 1991.

[31] Carlos Arribas, 'La Fallida Investigación a Jesús Losa', *El País*, 20 October 2009.

[32] Carlos Arribas, 'La Federación de Ciclismo Fichó Al Doctor Ferrari Para Dopar Al Equipo de Pista En Atlanta 96', *El País*, 17 April 2018.

[33] Eduardo Rodrigálvarez, 'La Enésima Batalla', *El País*, 16 December 2000.

[34] Carlos Arribas, 'El Juez Entrega Las Bolsas Pero Absuelve a Eufemiano y Labarta', *El País*, 15 June 2016.

one of the greatest doping scandals. Spanish doctors seem to have a profound knowledge of effective doping practices, most of them starting in the nineties, and Spanish authorities tend to privilege a nationalist stand when facing doping accusations.[35]

Barcelona's touristification hell

Finally, we must talk about the successful urban renewal of Barcelona. The opening of the city to the sea transformed the social life and improved leisure and transportation in the city. Thanks to newly constructed iconic buildings and the promotion boost of the Olympics, Barcelona became one of the favourite destinations of international tourism and one of the most economically dynamic cities. However, Barcelona's tourism success has finally become a problem. The service economy of Barcelona is not based on high-added value services, like biotechnology or big data, but on tourism. The gradual process of *touristification* and gentrification of the city has reached a critical point in recent years with the arrival of the companies of collaborative economy and holyday rentals. The impact of Airbnb and others has increased rentals 66.6% from 2013 to 2017.[36] The degradation of the city because of tourism was the main point in leftist Ada Colau's campaign, and her first measure after taking office was a moratorium on hotel licenses.[37] The growth of Barcelona has turned out to be unbalanced and unequal, probably the most unexpected and paradoxical consequence of those Games.[38]

Conclusion

The Olympic Games in Barcelona are one of the few games of the last forty years that have, in the eyes of public opinion, left an exemplary social, sporting and urban legacy. A legacy certainly different from the 2004 Games that led to the ruin of Greece, and that of Rio 2016, full of

---

[35] Rodrigo Pardo and Dominique Bodin, 'Análisis de Prensa de Los Casos de Dopaje de Marta Domínguez y Alberto Contador: ¿héroes o Villanos?', *Historia y Comunicacion Social* 17 (2012): 297–316.

[36] idealista.com, main real state Spanish webpage shows mean price went from 11.6 euros/m² to 17.5. Natalia Bravo, 'Así Ha Evolucionado El Alquiler En Barcelona En Los Últimos Diez Años', idealista.com, 2018 www.idealista.com/news/inmobiliario/vivienda/2018/03/01/764561-asi-ha-evolucionado-el-alquiler-en-barcelona-en-los-ultimos-diez-anos.

[37] Clara Blanchar, 'Barcelona Mayor Introduces One-Year Ban on New Tourist Accommodation', *El País*, 2 July 2015.

[38] Horacio Capel Saez, '¿En Qué Ha Fallado Barcelona?', *Finisterra, XLV, 90* XLV, no. 90 (2010): 173–204.

social unrest and abandoned facilities. It is true that Barcelona '92 allowed an urban regeneration and a new sports policy in Spain. Spanish democracy is now also comparable to the rest of European democracies and infinitely better than the National-Catholic dictatorship of General Franco. However, it is still true that the structural weaknesses of a project based on political amnesia and neoliberal modernization are clearly visible.

8

Women's League Hockey and its Early Development

Mark Evans

Abstract

With the setting up of The Hockey Association in 1886 and The All England Women's Hockey Association in 1895 the sport of hockey, like many other sports at this time, formalized rules and structures that helped to develop it into the sport we know today. However, unlike other sports such as rugby and football the history of the game has not attracted much interest. This is now beginning to change. The Hockey Museum, situated in Woking, is helping in this process and its many volunteers are helping to bring the history of the game to the fore. As one of these volunteers I have been looking at the issue of women's leagues and how they developed. The problems they caused for the women's establishment, the development of a second Association to look after the leagues, and the playing of international matches with Ireland and Scotland are just a few of the factors that make the story a fascinating one. In this chapter I take a look at these aspects. There are though many things still to consider, one of which is why the men did not follow the women's lead and set-up leagues in their game. Work for the future, no doubt. Now though, we consider how the early women's leagues began and what effect they had on the game of hockey.

Keywords: Women, Hockey, Leagues, Cup Competitions, Internationals.

Introduction

The development of women's league hockey is a subject that has not attracted much research, but it is a fascinating story and one that deserves further investigation. People within the hockey world believed that women's league hockey only really began in the late 1970's evolving into a national Premier competition in 1989/90. However, the first women's league in England was formed in 1910 in Manchester. This was followed by several other leagues, mainly in the North and Midlands. As we shall see many were very successful and yet despite the success of women's league hockey the men did not follow, and it was many years before they began playing league hockey. Why they resisted the lure of the leagues is not yet fully understood but I am sure many must have been tempted.

There is very little written material in relation to ladies' league hockey although Jo Halpin (2017) in her article 'Thus far and no farther: the rise of women's hockey leagues in England from 1910 to 1939' provides an insight into the subject up to 1939.[1] Local newspapers have proved to be the most useful source as several them carried articles on the leagues, usually weekly, in which there would be match reports, player profiles, results, league tables and often some comment by the reporter on what they regarded as important issues within the hockey world. Before we look more closely at these early leagues it is important to consider how hockey developed. Various forms of ball and stick games have been in existence for centuries. M.K. Howells in his book *A Centenary of Modern Hockey 1871 – 1971* gives an explanation into how the modern men's game developed.

In the early 1870 two versions of hockey were developing, one played by Blackheath with teams of 15 a-side using a black cube of solid rubber as the ball and the other played by Teddington Cricket Club, using a cricket ball as the ball.[2]

On 18 January 1886 six clubs, Teddington, Surbiton, Wimbledon, Ealing (later Mid Surrey), Molesey and Trinity College, Cambridge met at the Holborn Restaurant and formed the Hockey Association (H.A.). This became the men's governing body. Blackheath attended but could not persuade the other clubs to play their form of the game and they formed a Hockey Union with ten other clubs in 1887 which was dissolved in March 1895 with the Union clubs switching to the Association game.[3]

In the women's game Marjorie Pollard, in her booklet *Fifty Years of Women's Hockey* records that some form of hockey was being played at Oxford University around 1887. It was played with plain ash sticks and a string covered ball. Cambridge took up the game with the Newnham College Hockey Club being formed in 1890.

In Ireland the game was popular and the Irish Ladies' Hockey Union was formed in 1894. During the Christmas holidays of 1894–5, The Alexandra College, Dublin invited the Cambridge ladies to Ireland to play a series of matches. The English ladies returned with the intention of forming their own Association and after an international match of

---

[1] Jo Halpin 'Thus far and no farther': the rise of women's hockey leagues in England from 1910 to 1939, Sport in History, 37:2, 146-163, DOI: 10.1080/17460263.2017.1318089

[2] M. K. Howells, *A Centenary of Modern Hockey 1871 – 1971'*, 7 - 9

[3] Howells, *A Centenary of Modern Hockey*, 17.

sorts on April 10 they elected some officers. However, it was not until November 23, 1895, the first meeting of the Ladies' Hockey Association was held. In September 1896, the word Ladies was replaced with Women's and the title 'The All England Women's Hockey Association (A.E.W.H.A.) was adopted.[4]

The ladies tried to join the men's association, but they were informed by the hon secretary, Mr Stanley Christopherson that 'The Hockey Association had been formed entirely in the interests of men's clubs and that it could not officially recognise the existence of the new association'.[5] The refusal of the Hockey Association to allow the ladies to join led them to decide not to allow men to serve on their committees, a belief that they stuck to for many years and one that was to impact on the ladies' leagues that were soon to form. However, despite their differences, both associations were against playing in leagues and for cups. They believed in playing for the love of the sport. These friendly games were often arranged during the week when many people were working, restricting the number of people who could play. The hockey clubs formed were private clubs with membership fees which many could not afford and so in some areas of the country the number of hockey players was restricted.

In 1910, though, things in the ladies' hockey world changed when the first ladies' hockey league was formed in Manchester. The league seems to have been known by a few different names. The Lancashire and Cheshire Ladies Hockey League, Manchester and District Ladies Hockey League and the Ladies Hockey League are three of the titles I have seen. In the first season there were enough teams to form two leagues. The first division consisted of the following teams; Leigh, St Margaret's, Levenshulme, Saddleworth, Ashton, Urmston, Oldham, Clarendon, Clifton and Withington and in the second division teams from Holyrood, Leigh, Ashton, Dukinfield, Gorton, Levenshulme, Coldhurst, Oldham, Withington and Clifton competed.[6]

At the end of the season a presentation evening was held, a feature that became popular with women's leagues. *The Leigh Chronicle* reported on the night:

---

[4] Marjorie Pollard, *Fifty Years of Women's Hockey* (St Christopher Press Ltd, 1946), 5 – 6

[5] Pollard, *Fifty Years of Women's Hockey*, 6.

[6] 'Ladies' Hockey League', *The Chronicle*, February 17, 1911, 7.

The Ladies Hockey League has many enthusiastic members, and at their first gala, held at Belle Vue on Saturday, there were 1,500 spectators, mostly ladies. The League was formed at the beginning of this season by way of dissenting from the policy of the All England Women's Hockey Association, which is governed practically from the South of England. The new body is the only hockey league in existence, and despite the fact that in all other games prizes and trophies are played for the A.E.W.H.A. debarred from membership all clubs which have joined the League. This drastic procedure has, however, in no way deferred its progress, and the movement has spread over Lancashire, Yorkshire and Cheshire. During the last season 20 clubs, comprising 600 members, entered the competition and for next season sufficient applications have been received to form another division.[7]

The article highlights one of the main issues the leagues were to face. The A.E.W.H.A, initially barred the clubs that joined the league from membership. The relationship between the Association and the leagues was a difficult one from the start and it eventually led to the setting up of a second Association, who would help to support the leagues. Leigh were the first league champions and retained the title the following year.

The Leagues' first season had been a success, despite the A.E.W.H.A., and it continued to flourish. As yet it has not been possible to determine how long the league was in existence, but it was the springboard that saw the introduction of leagues in women's hockey. There was a second league in Manchester, known as the Manchester Sunday School League, but not much is known about this league, although we know in the 1937–1938 season both leagues played in the Northern Counties tournament, held at Scarborough. [8] Other leagues followed and currently there is evidence for twenty-two leagues in England, three leagues in Ireland and two in Scotland. Many of the leagues were in the industrial towns of South Lancashire, although, there were leagues in Yorkshire and the Midlands. I have chosen a few of these leagues to show how they were formed and how they developed.

1915 Bolton Sunday School Social League
In 1890, the Bolton Working Lads Club was formed with the aim 'to provide healthy and natural exercise and amusement for the working

---

[7] 'Ladies' Hockey', *The Chronicle*, April 7, 1911, 2.
[8] 'Ladies Hockey, Plans For Scarboro' Tournament', *Sports Special ('Green Un')*, December 18, 1937, 3.

lad'. By April 1894 it had become the Bolton Sunday School Social League, which is still in existence and is known as the Bolton Sports Federation. The ladies' hockey league was not one of the original members, but in March 1914 an article appeared in the local sports newspaper, *The Buff,* which reported on a meeting at Cheadles Restaurant where the Chairman of the Manchester league spoke,

> He said skirts must be 8/10 inches from the ground/goalkeepers to have cricket pads, others ankle guards/plain skirts looked better. Football rules apply.[9]

BOLTON'S CRACK HOCKEY TEAM.

FLETCHER STREET WESLEYANS
who won the Bolton S.S.S. League Championship last season.

Left to right. M. Bibby, E. Hudson, E. Green, N. Rigby, H. Johnson, M. Dickinson, C. Greenhalgh,
M. Rigby, E. Taylor (capt.), A. Howcroft, M. Whittle, E. Ashworth, E. Abbot, Edna Taylor,
J. Daniels, A. Booth.

Fig. 1. The first Bolton Sunday School Social League Champions - Fletcher Street Wesleyans 1915 – 1916.

This led to the Bolton Sunday School Social Ladies Hockey League being formed in 1915 and to them joining the Bolton Sunday School Social League. In the first season there were six teams, all from Church groups, like many other sports teams of the age. The league had 112 players signed on. The chair of the section and the secretary were both men, which as we have seen, the A.E.W.H.A. was not in favour of. Fletcher Street Wesleyans were the first Champions and in 1922 a Welfare section was formed enabling mill girls to participate in league hockey.[10] The

---

[9] *Bolton Sports Federation Ladies Hockey League Centenary Booklet,* 10.
[10] *Bolton Sports Federation Centenary Booklet.*

league is still in existence today and is the oldest surviving ladies hockey league in the country.

1917 Liverpool

A league was formed in Liverpool but there is some confusion as to whether it was formed in 1917 or 1918. Evidence from *The Lancashire Daily Post*, January 25th, 1939, indicates the date the Liverpool Ladies League was formed was 1917 as their hockey correspondent spoke to a long-standing player and administrator, Miss Seddon, about the long services of hockey players and she told the correspondent,

> …she was elected first match secretary of the Liverpool League when it was formed in 1917.[11]

The Liverpool Echo though in an article in 1948 refers to 'The Liverpool Ladies Hockey League, which was formed in 1918'.[12]

There may be some discussion about when the league was first formed, however, what is not in doubt as the *Liverpool Echo*'s correspondent 'Onlooker' in April 1927 reported is:

> …the eighty-odd clubs now playing under league auspices would ever be able to find regular bookings by themselves…the fact that the league is in existence has provided the incentive for the formation of new clubs who would certainly not have seen the light of Saturday afternoon otherwise. So, we can at least owe, to this big Liverpool Ladies Hockey League, the credit for increasing the personnel of the code a hundredfold.[13]

The league continued to develop and during the late 1930's had eight leagues. It was to become one of the more important leagues and John Leishman, the secretary of the League for a number of years, was one of the driving forces behind the setting up of a Leagues' Association.

1919 Farnworth and District Sunday Schools Ladies Hockey League

This was one of the smaller leagues that developed and though it only lasted for ten years it had a big impact in the area. Farnworth is on the outskirts of Bolton and the *Farnworth Weekly Journal and Observer*, carried weekly reports on the league. On August 23, 1929, however, it reported

---

[11] 'Hockey Notes', *The Lancashire Daily Post*, January 25, 1939, 9.
[12] 'Ladies Hockey League', *The Liverpool Echo*, August 17, 1948, 3.
[13] 'The Hockey Outlook', *Liverpool Football Echo*, April 23, 1927, 7.

on the sad demise of the league but indicated what the benefit had been to the ladies of Farnworth:

> It will be with much regret many of our readers will learn that the Farnworth Hockey League has ceased to function – at least for the present. A meeting was held during the week, when it was learned that only five Sunday schools could organize teams…They were not enough to run a league and so, although, the district has half-a-dozen other clubs functioning, it will for the time being take second place to other localities. The League…has done a great deal to encourage cleanliness in sport and given the girls an opportunity for exercise.[14]

It is not surprising the league only lasted for ten years as there were bigger leagues close by, including Bolton, which several teams joined after the leagues demise.

1921 Stockport and District

Championship Cup.
FIRST DIVISION.

Presented to the League by
Councillor JOHN GREENHALGH, Esq.

Fig. 2. Stockport and District Ladies Hockey League Championship Cup Presented to the winners of Division One of the League.

---

[14] *The Farnworth Weekly Journal and Observer*, August 23, 1929.

In a letter to the editors of the *Stockport Advertiser and the Stockport Express* Mr S. Dearden in March 1921 said:

> He had watched with pleasure the growing popularity of hockey in Stockport and the surrounding districts, and seeing that we as a town provide so well for all other sports, I shall be glad to enter into correspondence with any persons who are sufficiently interested in the game with a view to promoting a Ladies Hockey League in this district.[15]

A meeting was organized on April 14, 1921, and it was decided to form a league. The league began on 1 October 1921 with thirteen teams from a radius of seven miles of the town centre. The winners of the first league title were Stockport Adult School. In the second season there were two leagues with 670 registered players, an increase of 300 from the first. Cheadle Heath Junior Sports Club were the first division champions and Heaton Chapel St Andrew's were the second division champions.[16] It is believed the league continued until 2007 when the remaining teams joined together to form one club bringing the league to an end.

1930 Leyland and District Ladies Hockey League
The Leyland and District Ladies League was formed in 1930 but by 1932 it had become the Lancashire Central Ladies Hockey League. This league is still in existence. The league was forward looking and keen to improve the standard of play. In 1938 they looked at a coaching scheme involving the umpires, mainly men, acting as coaches. The Bolton League had a similar scheme and the idea was that the league would arrange supplementary games for players who were not picked for their team on Saturday and new players who would like to take up the game, where they would receive coaching from the umpires.[17] It is not known how successful this scheme was and whether it was actually put in place. It would be interesting to ask today's umpires, players and clubs what they thought about the scheme. Would it attract more players into the game? Would it improve the standard of play?

As with other leagues presentation evenings were an event to look forward to. The 1941 evening was no exception,

---

[15] *Stockport District Hockey League Hockey Record* (Seasons 1921-2, 1922-3), 2.
[16] *Stockport District Hockey League Hockey Record* (Seasons 1921-2, 1922-3), 7–11.
[17] 'Hockey Notes', *The Lancashire Daily Post*, December 28, 1938, 2.

> …the Lancashire Central Women's Hockey League trophies were presented at the annual dance at…Over 300 attended and a competition for 100 cigarettes raised £5 for the Red Cross.[18]

I am not sure if a raffle for 100 cigarettes would feature at any hockey presentation evening now! However, with over 300 guests it does show that these evenings were popular and an important part of the league calendar. Other Lancashire Leagues were formed including; Middleton and District Sunday Scholl Ladies Hockey League, Rochdale and District Ladies Hockey League, Wigan and District Hockey League, Leigh and District Ladies Hockey League, Bury and Radcliffe Ladies League, and Swinton and Pendlebury Ladies Hockey League.

Sheffield Ladies League – formed in 1919

The Yorkshire Post in June 2012 indicates when and how the Sheffield Ladies League was initially formed:

> The Sheffield and District Women's Hockey Association was founded from 'lowly beginnings' in 1919, when 10 hockey teams met in the corner of the hockey pitch at High Storrs Grammar School in Bents Green, Sheffield and decided to begin competing against each other.[19]

In 1922, the league changed its name to become the Sheffield and District Women's Hockey Association. It is not clear why League was replaced with Association, perhaps it was to please the A.E.W.H.A., as the Sheffield League arranged matches with Lancashire, Nottinghamshire, Lincolnshire and Derbyshire county elevens as well as matches with the Bradford and Leeds leagues.[20] There is also evidence for leagues in Leeds, Bradford, Hull, North Tyneside, Birmingham and Leicestershire.

The league system did not work for everyone though, as a report in the *Sports Special ('Green 'UN')* in 1920 points out. Their correspondent 'Sticks' notes that,

> at the last meeting of the North Lindsey Hockey League Committee, it was decided to alter the constitution of the body to that of an Association, thereby dropping a league table…The

---

[18] 'Women's Hockey', *The Lancashire Daily Post*, April 26, 1941, 3.

[19] *The Yorkshire Post*, June 15, 2012, page unknown.

[20] 'Sports and Pastimes', *The Sheffield Daily Telegraph*, Wednesday, September 27, 1922, 8.

committee…are also taking the initial steps towards the resuscitation of the Lincolnshire County Association.[21]

The new leagues consisted of a variety of teams. There were church teams and a number of the early leagues contain the title 'Sunday Schools Ladies Hockey League'. Works based teams were encouraged to join the leagues and the Bolton League had separate divisions, a Sunday School league and a Welfare or works league. This was in part as a result of a drive to raise moral during and after the First World War when many of the munitions factories and the other factories where women were being employed, had welfare officers coming in to encourage the setting up of sports teams. Dick Kerr's, for example, who played in the Central Lancashire League, were a successful hockey team but had a much more famous ladies football team. Schools were another source for teams. Girls had played hockey at school and wished to continue playing after leaving. The opportunities to join the established A.E.W.H.A. teams may not have been an option and so they formed their own school teams with ex-pupils and some current pupils playing.

There were other areas interested in setting up leagues although evidence to confirm their existence has not been found. In Burnley an article by 'a Lady Contributor' featured in *The Burnley News* on November 22, 1919,

> The Charlon Ladies' Hockey Club, which is being well supported, is now in its third season, and is still progressing. Already many matches are booked for this season, the match today (Saturday) being against the Bacup and Rawtenstall Secondary School. Perhaps in the near future one may see the formation of a Burnley Ladies' Hockey League. Why not?[22]

In Coventry, *The Midland Daily Telegraph* in 1921 published a letter from the captain of Daimler Hockey Club:

> Ladies Hockey League. Sir, - I was very pleased to see 'Enthusiast's' letter in your Monday evening's edition, which I am sure voiced the feelings of many ladies playing hockey in this district. If only a few keen ladies and gentleman could be brought together and a suitable person found with the necessary interest and ability to act as secretary, the success of such a league is

---

[21] The Hockey Field, 'By Sticks', *Sports Special ('Green 'UN')*, Saturday, October 9, 1920 6.

[22] Local Hockey Notes, *The Burnley News*, November 22, 1919, 5.

almost assured. Already there is a sufficient nucleus for a 'works league' in the ladies' teams already playing, as the published results in your Saturday night's edition testify. In addition, there are many ladies playing in 'mixed' teams who might be induced to run ladies' teams in connection with their offices and works with profit to themselves and other players of less ability. I trust as the results of this correspondence, something may be done in this way to foster outdoor sports of a suitable nature among the ladies of this city, and thus fill a long-felt need.[23]

Cup competitions

The A.E.L.H.A. was not only against teams playing in leagues, they did not want them playing in cup competitions. However, in these newly forming leagues, cup competitions became a major part of the season:

The Liverpool League compete for Messrs Lewis's Cup in the Senior Section, the Diamine Cup in the Intermediate Section and the Mrs. Arthur Moore's Cup in the Junior Section. The Bolton League compete for the J.F. Steele Cup in the 'A' Section, the Davenport Cup in the 'B' and a trophy presented for the newly formed 'C' Section. The Stockport League have their Senior and Junior Flags. The Lancashire Central League the Douglas Cup, the Wigan League the Swift Cup, the Leigh and District League the Arthur Crooke Shield and the Bury League the Rose Bowl competition.[24]

There were cups in other leagues; the Rochdale League played for the Turner Cup and the Kershaw Cup and the Sheffield League had the Sheffield Challenge Cup in which the first division teams were exempt. The Farnworth and District Sunday Schools Ladies Hockey competed for the Mitton Challenge Shield and I mention this Shield as it has recently been rediscovered after years of been hidden in a loft. The Bolton League were celebrating their centenary year and placed an advert in the local paper for items to help them celebrate the anniversary. One of the items they were offered was a shield which turned out to be the Mitton Challenge Shield. They took possession of it and, through the League Chair, I became aware of the Shield and began looking into its history.

---

[23] *The Midland Daily Telegraph*, March 16, 1921, page unknown.
[24] 'Hockey Notes', *Lancashire Daily Post*, January 11, 1939, 9.

The Farnworth Weekly Journal and Observer ('*The Journal*'), reported on the league and from these reports I was able to uncover the history of the competition. It only lasted for six years beginning in 1924 and finishing when the league disbanded in 1929. Hollands School were the most successful team winning the Shield on four occasions 1924, 1927, 1928 and 1929.

In the first year of the competition, Hollands School and Walkden St. Paul's, made the final. The match was played at Hill Top, the ground of one of the other league teams, Wesley Hall. Both teams were well supported, and a record crowd turned out to watch what was to

Fig. 3. The Mitton Challenge Shield (The Hockey Museum, Woking)

become a controversial final. *The Journal* carried a report of the game, which after 70 minutes had finished 1 – 1.

> It was at this stage there was a dramatic turn of events which changed a splendidly fought contest into a complete fiasco. The rules governing the competition state that 'failing a definite result being arrived at the end of the usual seventy minutes' play, twenty minutes extra time must be played'. It was the extra time Walkden St. Paul's refused to play. The referee whistled for the commencement of the extra period, but Walkden would not toe the line with the result that the referee again blew his whistle, Holland's went away, scored a goal, and in this way became the first holders of the Shield.[25]

The game caused some controversy and *The Journal* received several letters about the match. A representative of Walkden St. Paul's, J. Twist, wrote to the paper providing an explanation for the action of the team. He explained that the decision was taken by the club's officials and that they had no intention of breaking the rules and he was not sure they had as he claimed there was no rules about extra time:

---

[25] Farnworth Hockey League Challenge Shield Fiasco, *The Farnworth Weekly Journal and Observer* May 2, 1924

We considered that having played a game of so vigorous a nature, we had no right to expect them to continue further. I take it that in fostering games for our girls we are out for recreation which means re-creation – the art of recreating, amusing, or refreshing spirits or strength after toil. If we are going to ask them to overtax their physical powers, then we fail in our object, as they are thereby rendered less capable of fulfilling their other duties in life. I think all fair-minded people would agree that the physical powers of the female are not the equal of the male, and as many of the players were showing signs of distress in the interests of true sport we called 'enough'.[26]

The explanation expresses a view of women's sport that was widely held at the time. What current women players would think of the views expressed would be interesting to find out. There is no comment about what the members of the team thought about the decision, if in fact they were even asked.

The English Ladies Hockey Leagues Association.
Leagues were now successfully established and flourishing in the North. Was hockey going to go the same way as rugby and divide into two codes? The formation of the leagues had brought a problem for the ladies' hockey hierarchy, the A.E.W.H.A. They were against leagues and cup competitions, although strangely enough, they were happy for university teams and school teams to play some forms of competitive hockey. They initially refused to allow membership to the teams who had joined the Manchester League and for a number of years discussion and debate about how to deal with the league teams ensued. The Association eventually allowed some league teams to join but the relationship was never a happy one. We know some leagues were affiliated to county associations and their league teams were regarded as 'counties' and could compete as counties in competitions.[27] However, some of the leagues wanted to have more control and eventually they formed a second association, the English Ladies Hockey Leagues Association (E.L.H.L.A.) in 1932. The Liverpool League was one of the main movers in the development of this new Association and their secretary John Leishman, was one of the main supporters.

Their main objective, as noted in the *Lancashire Daily Post*, in 1933 was 'the organization of competitive games in which no distinction, save

---

[26] 'The Hockey Final', *Farnworth Weekly Journal and Observer*, May 9, 1924.
[27] 'On the Hockey Field, Looking After The Women's League Interests; A New Association', *The Liverpool Echo*, March 19, 1932, 7.

that of excellence in the field, can aid the player who is desirous of gaining the game's highest honours'.[28] *The Sports Special ('Green Un')* named the leagues who joined the new Association, Liverpool, Manchester Sunday School, Lancashire Central, Stockport and Middleton and made the point,

> All these, it will be noted, are in South Lancashire, so that the title, to say the least, is a trifle misleading.[29]

This was true, and despite its aims, the Association could never attract leagues outside Lancashire and Cheshire to join. Why this was so is not known and requires further research. The article lists what the new Association was hoping to offer to the leagues who joined,

> The programme, as set forth in the last general meeting, provides for an Easter Tournament and also a competition for an English Cup, while an international game against an Irish team was mooted...'[30]

Easter tournament

Was the Association able to deliver on what it had set out? The first Easter tournament was held in Manchester in 1933 and was for league clubs. The tournament was to be over two days and teams from leagues in Manchester, Stockport, Liverpool and the Lancashire Central League entered A trophy had been donated by Sir Benjamin Johnson and Balshaw's, Diamond, Pemberton, Bramhall and Leigh, all prominent teams in their respective leagues entered.[31] However, the format of the tournament changed and teams containing the best players in the leagues, chosen by league committees, competed as league teams for the E.C. Caley Trophy. Exactly why and when it changed is not known. When the E.L.H.L.A. disbanded in the early sixties, the trophy was given to the Lancashire Central League who still play for it. E.C. Caley was the first President of the E.L.H.L.A. and so it is possible the trophy was renamed in her honour or she donated it.

---

[28] 'Women's Hockey', The Lancashire Daily Post, 23 February 1933, 11.

[29] 'In the Women's Hockey World, Sports Special', ('Green Un'), Saturday, October 22, 1932, 6.

[30] Ibid

[31] 'Women Who Play Many Parts Prominent Players', The Lancashire Daily Post, April 6, 1933 p10

The English Cup

The English Cup was introduced in 1934 and teams in the different leagues affiliated to the Association played against each other. An article in *The Lancashire Daily Post* confirmed where the Cup originated.

> The draw for the first round of the English Hockey Cup to be played on November 6th takes place tonight. The competition is played under the auspices of the English Ladies Hockey League Association to whom the cup was presented in 1934 by Mr. Frederick Johnson of Liverpool. Leyland Motors were the first winners beating Liverpool Olympic in the final as they did the following year. The present holders are Stockport.[32]

Little was known about the Cup and in fact the Hockey Museum, when they received an enquiry about it in 2015, doubted its existence. The enquiry had been sent by Alan Lancaster who had two pictures, one a team photograph, which Alan thought was Newhey Ladies Hockey team. One of the players was holding a cup, which was believed to be the English Cup. In the photograph were his mother Doreen Howles and her two sisters, Vera and June. The second photograph was of the three sisters with the Cup.

Enquires revealed that Newhey had won the Cup in the 1950-1951 season defeating Poynton in the final 1–0 with Vera Simpson, one of Alan's aunts scoring the winning goal in the first half. A report in the *Rochdale Observer* states the match was 'played almost entirely in hail and rainstorms' but declares that Newhey were 'worthy winners of a very hard game'. It also hints that the Association were struggling for money as, although the cup was presented by the Association's treasurer, Mr W. Wood, 'the finances of the Association do not allow them to give medals'.[33] One of the most successful teams was Leyland Motors, from the Central Lancashire League, who won the Cup on at least eight occasions. Cheadle Heath were another successful side winning the Cup on at least three occasions and finishing runners up on two.

It is believed the tournament ended in the early sixties when the E.L.H.L.A. disbanded. Recently, though, the granddaughter of John Lishman, Ailna Martin, has found new information indicating that the Cup was given to the Central Lancashire League and was renamed the

---

[32] 'Hockey Notes', *The Lancashire Daily Post*, October 20, 1937, 9
[33] 'Ladies Hockey, English Cup comes to Newhey', *The Rochdale Observer*, April 11, 1951.

Lishman Cup in recognition of the work her grandfather did for women's league hockey. Although the original Cup has been replaced with a new Cup it is still being played for by teams in the Central Lancashire League. A history of the Cup is held at the Hockey Museum in Woking.

International matches
The third aim for the Association was to provide international matches and as with the other two they delivered. The initial plan was to play Ireland as reported in the *Lancashire Daily Post*,

> The honorary secretary Mr. John Lishman reported that negotiations were going forward to arrange an international match between this association and Ireland during the season 1932–33.[34]

However, these negotiations fell through, although games were later arranged with Ireland, and the first 'international match' was a match against Scotland which was played in Glasgow on March 4, 1933 with England winning 2–1. These international matches continued during the 1930's. Team selection could sometimes cause debate. In 1937, at the end of the tournament for the E.S. Caley Trophy, the Central Lancashire team, who had won, played the England team chosen to play against Scotland and defeated them 1–0.[35] In 1939, England faced Scotland at Cheadle Heath Sports Ground. They had already defeated Northern Ireland 7–0 on Easter Monday and five days later they defeated Scotland 4–1 and as *The Stockport Express* reported were presented with a trophy which had been donated by 'Mrs. A Moores, of Liverpool, to be competed for by the Irish Union, Scottish and English Leagues'.[36]

It appears that after the start of the Second World War these games were suspended and replaced with games between an English Leagues team and The Rest team in aid of the British Red Cross. I have come across evidence for games in 1940 and 1944. At the present time it is unclear if the international matches continued after the War. How these international matches were viewed by others within the ladies game is not known. We do know that playing in goal for the English League team was Mary Tattlock, who went on to play for the A.E.W.H.A. and have a very distinguished career. She started playing in goal for St.

---

[34] 'English Ladies Hockey', *The Lancashire Daily Post*, July 11, 1932.
[35] 'Hockey Notes', *The Lancashire Daily Post*, April 7, 1937, 9.
[36] 'International Women's Hockey in Stockport', *Stockport Express*, April 20, 1939.

Matthews, and then Francis St. Farnworth, both teams in the Bolton League. She then moved to Prestwich in the Manchester League and played her first international against Scotland on March 13th 1954 at Wembley. She gained 44 caps conceding less than a dozen goal.[37] The new Association had managed to achieve three of its main aims. The Association continued into the early sixties when it disbanded. Why and exactly when this happened is yet to be uncovered.

Inter-League games
Inter League games were to become an important part of ladies league hockey. Some of the earliest inter-league games were between Manchester and Sheffield and Sheffield and Bradford. The games were popular, and teams were chosen by the league committees with a number of leagues putting out second elevens. In 1939, a match between Bolton and Bury at the Eagley Mills ground in Bolton attracted over 300 spectators. A report on the match in the *Liverpool Daily Post* also notes the involvement of the E.L.H.L.A.,

> Always an attractive fixture, Saturday's game was the first time the two Leagues had met under the auspices of the English Ladies' Hockey Leagues' Association.[38]

It is clear that the E.L.H.L.A. worked hard to develop league hockey and it is only really now that its importance is beginning to be understood. The relationship it had with the A.E.W.H.A. is fascinating and gives an insight into twentieth-century values. I have tried to provide an introduction into how ladies league hockey developed and some of the problems it faced but there is still a lot to uncover about how the leagues influenced the game. Eventually, I hope to be able to tell the full story of the impact they had on women's hockey and highlight some of the figures who were responsible for encouraging many women to play a game they may otherwise never have played.

---

[37] *Bolton Sports Federation Ladies Hockey League Centenary Booklet*, 11.
[38] 'Women's Hockey Notes', *Liverpool Daily Post*, January 25, 1939, 11.

9

Pedestrian Six-day Races in Scotland 1878-1888

Derek Martin

Abstract

In the last quarter of the nineteenth century amateur athletics eclipsed professional athletics ('pedestrianism'). Whilst the amateur game absorbed short- and middle-distance events from pedestrianism it had no place for the multi-day, ultradistance events which had been a persistent presence in the professional sport since the eighteenth century. The 1870s and 1880s saw a short but intense blossoming of this old tradition in the shape of six-day races. Big races in Britain and America are referred to in the historiography of the sport but this paper looks at the so far unexamined smaller events in one region, Scotland, and notes particularly the part played by female pedestrians.

Keywords: Sport; Pedestrianism; Nineteenth century; Scotland; Women.

Introduction

Pedestrianism (competitive walking or running) was a major sport from the eighteenth century onward. In the typical pedestrian match each party wagered and it was of little interest whether he was a professional dependant on winnings for an income, or a 'gentleman amateur' merely betting to add excitement to the contest. Spectators were a welcome but not a necessary element – enclosed grounds were rare and therefore gate money was not an element in financing the contest. By the second quarter of the nineteenth century professional runners (gentleman amateurs had largely disappeared) were raising finance for their events through the mediation of a sophisticated network of pubs and hotels, where potential backers could meet pedestrians and which by the middle of the century were often provided the enclosed grounds where the contests were held. A vigorous sporting press provided the means of exchanging information amongst the pedestrians and their backers nationally and provided a public with the facts, stories and statistics that by the middle of the century had created a wide fan base.

The majority of events were sprints or middle-distance races but from the earliest days of the sport there had been also specialist long-distance pedestrians. The greatest of the gentleman amateurs, Captain Barclay

(1799-1854), walked 1,000 miles in 1,000 hours in 1809 and had popularized the idea of race walkers covering unfeasibly long distances against the clock for a wager. Professional pedestrians adopted the idea and there were periodically bouts of public enthusiasm for this branch of the sport. By the last quarter of the nineteenth century the spectacle of a single pedestrian walking for days on end against a time limit was rarely to be seen but, against all expectation, the 1870s and 1880s saw the phenomenal rise and fall of the six-day race.

Unusually, two specific individuals can plausibly be credited with the creation of this event. The first was an American, Edward Payson Weston (1839-1929). He came to public notice by walking the 478 miles from Boston to Washington in ten days in 1861 to attend Lincoln's first inauguration. By increasingly arduous walks over the next fifteen years, and assiduous self-publicity, he made ultradistance walking a financially viable enterprise. After his landmark achievement of walking 500 miles in six days at Newark, New Jersey he arrived in Britain in 1876, looking for new worlds to conquer. The British and Irish long-established culture of race walking was in the doldrums. Weston brought with him important ideas – that people could again be persuaded to watch very long races, that they could be held *indoors* and that money could be made from them.

In 1876, Weston toured the country giving exhibition walks of fifty to four hundred miles, to great enthusiasm. He attracted the notice of Sir John Astley (1828-1894), perhaps the last sporting baronet in the Regency mould, who took Weston as his protégé and put up his own money to promote big races in indoor venues for substantial money prizes. The first 'classic' six-day races (day and night from midnight Sunday to the following Saturday night) were promoted by Astley from 1877 at the Agricultural Hall in Islington, London, a large exhibition space which became the premier English venue for these races. The prospect of big rewards led to the development of a cohort of accomplished endurance athletes and unofficial world championships took place in London and New York.[1] Other big races were held in England in provincial towns and cities, notably at Sheffield, Manchester, Bristol and Lincoln. The six-day boom continued for almost

---

[1] The 'Astley Belt' contests as they were known were: March 1878 in London (O'Leary, 520 miles), *The Sportsman*, March 25, 1878, 3; October 1878 in New York (O'Leary, 408 miles), *New York World*, October 9, 1878, 3; March 1879 in New York (Rowell, 500 miles), *Boston Post*, March 17, 1878, 2; June 1879 in London (Weston, 550 miles), *Reynold's Newspaper*, June 22, 1879, 8; September 1879 in New York (Rowell, 524 miles), *Sporting Life*, October 1, 1879, 3.

a decade, but rapidly declined and petered out by the end of the 1880s and these races were largely forgotten until rediscovered in the 1960s and have begun to attract some attention in the literature.[2] But so far there has been no recognition of the nature, and indeed the existence of, smaller scale events away from the metropolitan areas. This paper attempts an assessment of how they operated in one such area, Scotland.

The Scottish events
The sporting press and the Scottish press were searched to identify multi-day races. Fifty-nine were identified between 1878 and 1888: one in 1878, thirteen in 1879, twenty-one in 1880, four in 1881, three in 1882, then no more contests until seventeen in the three years 1886 to 1888 (*see* Tables). Fifteen different towns and cities held races and there were over five hundred starters in all races combined.

The first six-day events were solo affairs. Weston walked four times in Scotland in the old pedestrian format of a set distance in a given time. He first attempted 500 miles in six days at the Royal Gymnasium, Edinburgh in June 1876, and twice more in 1877, and in February 1878 he walked for three weeks at Glasgow, covering 1,064 miles.[3] The first multi-day race in Scotland was in August 1878 at Edinburgh, a one-to-one challenge, between the Scot Peter M'Kellan and an experienced English pedestrian, William Howes. They walked fourteen hours a day for six days and attracted a crowd of three thousand by the last day.[4] There were another forty races over the next two and a half years (*see* Table 1). In early 1879 there were four events in Glasgow, organized by the pedestrians themselves, attempting to cash in on the publicity that was being generated by the London and New York events. The Glasgow events were also held indoors and were continuous for the whole six days. They were not a success, they were poorly organized, only two of them went the full length, the other two finishing prematurely in

---

[2] *See* John A. Lucas, 'Pedestrianism and the Struggle for the Sir John Astley Belt, 1878-1879', *Research Quarterly* 39(3) (October 1968): 587; Thomas J. Osler and Edward L. Dodd, 'Six-Day Pedestrian Races', *Annals of the New York Academy of Sciences* 301(1) (1977): 853; Osler, Dodd, *Ultra-Marathoning: The Next Challenge* (Mountain View: World Publications, 1979); John Cumming, *Runners and Walkers: A Nineteenth Century Sports Chronicle* (Chicago: Regnery Gateway, 1981); P. S. Marshall, *King of the Peds* (Milton Keynes: AuthorHouse, 2008); Matthew Algeo, *Pedestrianism: When Watching People Walk was America's Favorite Sport* (Chicago: Chicago Review Press, 2014).

[3] *Edinburgh Evening News*, June 26, 1876, 2 (450 miles); *Glasgow Herald*, February 19, 1877, 4 (330 miles); *Falkirk Herald*, March 17, 1877, 3 (422½ miles); *Bradford Daily Telegraph*, 25 February 1878, 3 (1,064 miles).

[4] *The Referee*, September 1878, 6.

disputes over gate money.

date	place	venue	days	hrs	M/F	starts
1878, 26 Aug.	Edinburgh	Royal Gymnasium	6	84	m	2
1879, 2 Jan.	Aberdeen	Concert Hall	3	48	m	15
1879, 21 Apr.	Glasgow	National Halls	2	142	m	2
1879, 19 May	Glasgow	Albion Halls	6	130	m	2
1879, 23 Jun.	Glasgow	Crown Hall	6	142	m	3
1879, 30 Jun.	Glasgow	National Halls	6	142	m	2
1879, 7 Jul.	Aberdeen	Recreation Ground	6	26	m	8
1879, 24 Jul.	Elgin	enclosed field	3	12	m	5
1879, 18 Aug.	Dundee	Newsome's Circus	6	72	m	10
1879, 6 Oct.	*Glasgow*	*Crown Hall*	*6*	*72*	*f*	*2*
1879, 6 Nov.	Perth	Drill Hall	3	50	m	11
1879, 15 Dec.	Dundee	Cooke's Circus	6	72	m	18
1879, 29 Dec.	Aberdeen	Cooke's Circus	6	72	m	11
1879, 30 Dec.	Perth	Drill Hall	2	24	m	19
1880, 9 Feb.	Aberdeen	Cooke's Circus	6	72	m	16
1880, 19 Feb.	Inverurie	Drill Hall	3	16	m	4
1880, 23 Feb.	Glasgow	Newsome's Circus	6	72	m	12
1880, 8 Mar.	Perth	Drill Hall	6	12	m	12
1880, 8 Mar.	Aberdeen	Burgh Hall	2	5	m	6
1880, 29 Mar.	Edinburgh	Royal Gymnasium	6	12	m	8
1880, 30 Mar.	Forfar	Reid Hall	3	15	m	5
1880, 14 Apr.	Montrose	the New Market	4	15	m	7
1880, 1 Jun.	Arbroath	ground	5	18	m	6
1880, 7 Jun.	Dundee	Cooke's Circus	6	12	m	11
1880, 21 Jun.	Aberdeen	Recreation Ground	6	26	m	14
1880, 22 Jun.	Alloa	Corn Exchange	5	18	m	7
1880, 19 Jul.	Falkirk	Town Hall	6	18	m	11
1880, 5 Aug.	Forfar	enclosed field	2	14	m	5
1880, 18 Sep.	Montrose	the New Market	3	6	m	5
1880, 20 Sep.	Crieff	Masons' Hall	6	21	m	6
1880, 20 Sep.	Dunfermline	Music Hall	6	21	m	7
1880, 27 Sep.	Dundee	Cooke's Circus	6	21	m	13
1880, 30 Oct.	Montrose	the New Market	3	6	m	10
1880, 4 Dec	Dundee	Cooke's Circus	7	65	m	18
1880, 28 Dec.	Falkirk	Town Hall	6	26	m	6
1881, 24 Jan.	Arbroath	warehouse	6	18	m	16
1881, 12 Mar.	Dundee	Cooke's Circus	7	65	m	18
1881, 20 Jun.	Aberdeen	Recreation Ground	6	26	m	6
1881, 2 Jul	Glasgow	Albion Hall	7 ·	65	m	10
1882, 8 Apr.	Dundee	Cooke's Circus	6	60	m	9
1882, 8 Apr.	*Dundee*	*Cooke's Circus*	*6*	*10*	*f*	*2*
1882, 6 May	Aberdeen	Recreation Grounds	7	26	m	8

Table 1. Multi-day pedestrian events in Scotland 1878-82.[5]

---

[5] Sources: *Aberdeen Journal* 1878-88; *Banffshire Journal* 1879; *Dundee Advertiser* 1879-88; *Dundee Courier* 1879-87; *Dundee Evening Telegraph* 1879-82; *Falkirk Herald*

The Glasgow events had displayed one of the sins of pedestrianism, the ever-present possibility of corruption. The big national and international events were 'clean', if only because they were professionally organized, and profits were dependant on attracting a mixed audience with a good proportion of newcomers to the sport who might be tempted in by the publicity and the novelty of indoor racing.

On 2 January 1879 a 48-hour event was held in Aberdeen that showed how the new event could be re-engineered to be more attractive to those audiences. It was promoted by the Bon-Accord Gymnastic Club, who had hired the city's concert hall (known as the Music Hall) on Union Street to give Aberdeen a taste of the 'tournaments which have of late attracted so much attention in the south'.[6] Starting at nine o'clock on Thursday evening and continuing until Saturday evening. The members of the Club diverted the audience with 'feats on the trapeze and horizontal bar' and attracted upwards of 4,000 spectators, including 'many well-known business and professional men and a considerable number of ladies'. There were 15 starters, all Scots, and the winner of £10 (say £1,000 today) was Willie Smith of Paisley with a total of 158 miles.

After this race promoters experimented constantly with the format - fourteen hours a day or twelve, or six or four, and anything from two to eight days. Aberdeen's next race, in July 1879 was six days, but four hours each evening Monday to Friday and six hours on Saturday (total 26 hours). The tactic of having racing only in the evenings paid off - on the second night there were 1,000 spectators and by Friday 2,000. The winner was George Noremac (*né* Cameron) of Edinburgh, who was to become one of the great six-day walkers and second was a local runner, Joe Leith, who had also come second in the New Year race.[7] A week later Elgin, sixty miles north of Aberdeen, a town with an annual Highland games put on an open-air three-night, 12 hour race that attracted few spectators.[8] Three weeks later Aberdeen's great rival, Dundee put on a six-day, 14 hours a day. The Dundee Sporting Club's entrepreneurial secretary, John Hagan, enlisted the *Sporting Life* to provide the referee, timekeeper and chief scorer and select the entrants. First prize was £50 and second £20. The venue was a circus building, Newsome's Circus by the docks, which meant a lap of only 48 yards and a dizzying 36 laps to

---

1880; *Glasgow Evening Citizen*, 1879; *Montrose, Arbroath and Brechin Review* 1888; *Peterhead Sentinel* 1888; *Sporting Life* 1879-88.
[6]*Aberdeen Journal*, January 2, 1879, 2.
[7] *Dundee Courier*, July 15, 1879, 5.
[8] *Banffshire Journal*, July 29, 1879, 6; August 5, 1879, 6.

the mile. The ten starters included eight southerners, all experienced long-distance men. The two Scots were Pat M'Kellan of Edinburgh and yet again Joe Leith the Aberdeen drover. At the finish on Saturday night a packed house saw southerner Sam Day win with 402 miles (14,447 circuits of the circus ring).[9]

In November in Perth, another of the East Coast towns, there was a three-day, 50-hour, tournament, in a drill hall, thirty laps to the mile. The first prize of £10 went to Joe Leith and second place (£2 only) to Peter M'Kellan.[10] Over New Year Dundee, Aberdeen and Perth put on well-supported races. *Bell's Life* treated the news with metropolitan condescension, 'these exhibitions are', they commented, 'happily, for all concerned save the promoters, gradually losing their hold on the metropolitan public, [but] they still find favour in the eyes of provincials ... this time luckily in far distant Dundee'.[11] But *Bell's Life* were perhaps influenced by the fact that their rival *The Sporting Life* was providing the officials . Dundee gave a £50 first prize and attracted eighteen starters, making a seriously crowded fifty-yard lap at Cooke's Circus. The event started with an impressive 70 miles by Willie Smith of Paisley on the first day (twelve hours), and an appreciative audience packed the house every night of the week, with perhaps 2,000 present at the finish.[12] Hagan of the Dundee Sporting Club extended his operations to Aberdeen and only eight days later held another six-day, 12 hours a day event there, also with a top prize of £50, this time entry restricted to Scots.[13] A New Year holiday crowd was attracted, audiences were large and 'enthusiastic', Smith finishing the winner on 347 miles.[14]

The following year, 1880, was the peak year for six-day races throughout Great Britain, around forty altogether, with twenty-one of them in Scotland (*see* Table 1). In 1881 and 1882 the big money races were in America, in England there were only a few big races, in Sheffield and Birmingham. In Scotland the smaller venues and shorter races dropped out and only the bigger races remained – three in Dundee, one in Arbroath (near Dundee), two in Aberdeen and one in Glasgow. After a

---

[9] *Dundee Evening Telegraph*, August 16, 1879, 4; *Dundee People's Journal*, August 23, 1879, 6; *Sporting Life*, August 27, 1879, 4.

[10] *Dundee Evening Telegraph*, November 10, 1879, 4.

[11] *Bell's Life*, December 20, 1879, 3.

[12] *Bell's Life*, December 20, 1879, 3; *Dundee Courier*, December 16, 1879, 5; December 22, 1879, 2.

[13] Robson of Liverpool, despite declaring his allegiance to Berwick-upon-Tweed on the entry form, was disqualified from fourth place for not being Scottish, but the spectators raised a subscription for him (*Bell's Life*, January 10, 1880, 9).

[14] *Sporting Life*, January 3, 1880, 3.

seven day, 26-hour in Aberdeen in May 1882, tournaments in Scotland stopped until 1886. When tournaments did revive in Scotland it was *female* pedestrians that the spectators came to see.

Female pedestrians

In March 1882 in Dundee, after a successful seven day, 65-hour race that had attracted 18 starters, the Sporting Club advertised another six-day contest at Cooke's Circus - 'Great Male and Female Pedestrian Tournament'. When the Circus realised that a women's race to be included, they applied to the Sheriff Court to have it stopped. They had never imagined, they said, that such a thing was contemplated; it was contrary to good morals, injurious to their reputation and would attract spectators 'of an objectionable kind'. [15] The claim was apparently dropped, and the race went ahead.

date	place	venue	days	hrs	M/F	starts
1886, 20 Feb.	*Aberdeen*	*Bon Accord Recreation Hall*	*7*	*16*	*f*	*7*
1886, 20 Mar.	Dundee	Newsome's Circus	7	16	f	7
1886, 27 Mar.	Aberdeen	Bon Accord Recreation Hall	7	21	m	26
1886, 5 Apr.	*Glasgow*	*National Hall*	*6*	*16½*	*f*	*4*
1886, 1 May	Aberdeen	Bon Accord Recreation Hall	7	14	f	13
1886, 26 Jun.	*Dundee*	*football/athletic ground*	*7*	*14*	*f*	*5*
1886, 10 Jul.	Aberdeen	Recreation Ground	7	14	f	13
1886, 31 Dec.	*Aberdeen*	*Bon Accord Recreation Hall*	*8*	*16*	*f*	*15*
1887, 10 Dec.	Forfar	Drill Hall	3	6	m	7
1888, 16 Feb.	Montrose	the New Markets	3	6(?)	m	6
1888, 26 Apr.	Peterhead	fish-curing yard	3	6	m	9
1888, 10 May	Peterhead	fish-curing yard	3	6	m	10
1888, 24 May	Peterhead	fish-curing yard	3	6	m	22
1888, 7 Jun.	Peterhead	*fish-curing yard*	3	6	f	13
1888, 14 Jun.	Peterhead	fish-curing yard	3	6	m	15
1888, 3 Sep.	Aberdeen	Bon Accord Recreation Hall	6	36	m	4
1888, 11 Sep.	*Aberdeen*	*Bon Accord Recreation Hall*	*2*	*3*	*f*	*2*

Table 2. Multi-day pedestrian events in Scotland 1878-88.[16]

The Circus should not have been shocked by the idea of female pedestrians. In fact, this was not a unique event. It would not be the first women-only race, or indeed even the first in Scotland. Back in 1879 at a hall on Sauchiehall Street in Glasgow Kate Brown and Janet Day had

---

[15] *Dundee Courier*, April 8, 1882, 2.
[16] Sources: *Aberdeen Journal* 1878-88; *Banffshire Journal* 1879; *Dundee Advertiser* 1879-88; *Dundee Courier* 1879-87; *Dundee Evening Telegraph* 1879-82; *Falkirk Herald* 1880; *Glasgow Evening Citizen*, 1879; *Montrose, Arbroath and Brechin Review* 1888; *Peterhead Sentinel* 1888; *Sporting Life* 1879-88.

contested a six-day, 72-hour race.[17] Women had a history of walking solo ultradistance matches going back almost to the days of Barclay.[18] There had been a resurgence in the 1870s and by the time of the Dundee race in 1882 female pedestrianism was an accepted part of the sporting scene and there were several well-established practitioners. Two of them had entered the Dundee race, 'Madame Englo', arguably the best of the English pedestriennes, and Kate Brown, who had won the match at Glasgow in October 1879. They walked for an hour and a half each evening, the men having already occupied the track for ten hours. The fears of 'objectionable' spectators were not fulfilled and the organizers' tactics were vindicated. They drew 'a large audience [and] greatest enthusiasm prevailed, [with] perfect order and decorum'.[19]

Nevertheless, it was almost four years until the six-day races reappeared in Scotland. The men had largely abandoned the event by now, and when there was a revival in 1886 it was almost entirely driven by the women. There were seven women-only tournaments, four at Aberdeen, two at Dundee and one in Glasgow (*see* Table 2). There were 60 starters in all. Female pedestrians had busied themselves in England (nearly all of whom were by now based in London) and seven leading professionals pedestrians from England made up the majority of the competitors in the first four Scottish competitions of 1886. In February 1886 Aberdeen offered £60 in prize money, £25 for first, second £15 and third £10 for a seven day, 16-hour walking contest, just two or three hours per night.[20] The organizers had imported five 'London ladies', who arrived on Friday, having suffered sea sickness on the thirty-six hour steamer voyage to Aberdeen. The recreation hall (which had a generous 195-yard wooden track) was crowded on Saturday evening: there were said to be 5,000 spectators when the first three-hour session began. Predictions that such a spectacle would 'shock the propriety of an Aberdeen audience' could be disregarded by now and 'even the

---

[17] *Glasgow Evening Citizen,* October 11, 1879, 3.
[18] See generally on male and female Barclayists, Derek Martin, 'A Short History of the Barclay Match: Long-Distance Pedestrianism in the Nineteenth Century', in *Sporting Cultures: Global Perspectives,* ed. Piercy and Oldfield (Manchester: MMU Sport and Leisure History, 2019), 149; Dahn Shaulis, 'Pedestriennes: Newsworthy but Controversial Women in Sporting Entertainment', *Journal of Sports History* 26(1) (1999): 29; Roberta J. Park, 'Contesting the Norm: Women and Professional Sports in Late Nineteenth-Century America', *International Journal of the History of Sport* 29(5) (2012): 730; Harry Hall, *The Pedestriennes: America's Forgotten Superstars* (Indianapolis, 2014).
[19] *Dundee Courier* April 10, 1882, 2.
[20] *Aberdeen Journal,* February 22, 1886, 3.

ladies of Aberdeen [had] turned out'.[21] Two unknown local women, Lizzie Reith and 'Miss Lorimer', shared the lead, made sixteen miles in the three hours, kept the southerners at bay for the remaining six sessions and came home in an exciting finish neck and neck, Reith winning by half a yard and so scooped between them £40 of the prize money. The novelty of the event, the 'home and away' rivalry and the (perhaps planned) closeness of the contest produced another capacity crowd.[22]

Predictably, the Aberdeen race was followed three weeks later (20 March) by a very similar event in Dundee (same total prize money, same duration) on the 42-yard lap Newsomes's Circus track. Miss Lorimer, who had been second in Aberdeen, this time picked up the £20 prize ahead of Madame Lucelle of Dudley, who had come fourth at Aberdeen; the Misses Randall, Letitia Brown and Leslie, all of London, picked up minor prizes. [23] Another five women's races followed in quick succession. A week after Dundee the four southerners moved to Glasgow for a six day, 16-hour event, where they shared £50 in prizes.[24] But at Glasgow there was no local opposition. When they moved back to Aberdeen for a 14-hour event starting 1 May they were again up against Miss Lorimer and Miss Reith, who had beaten them there in February. The southern contingent was now strengthened by Kate Brown and probably the best ultradistance walker at the time, Madame Englo from Brighton, but they were completely overwhelmed by local walkers. Miss Jeffrey of Aberdeen took the £20 first prize (for eighty-three miles) and the rest of the £60 prize money also went to Aberdonians; the best that the visiting pedestrians could manage was eighth (Miss Leslie with 71 miles).[25] The pattern was the same in June at Dundee: Miss Jeffrey won again (76 miles), with Englo second and Lorimer third.[26] In July at Aberdeen in a outdoor 14-hour race Miss Jeffrey again won the first prize (£15) and the best southern walker was Englo, sixth (£3) with 69 miles.[27] In the last race of the year, at Aberdeen in December, three southerners, Englo, Lucelle and Leslie, made a last attempt at the £15 first prize but it again went to Jeffrey (100 miles in an eight-day, 16 hour match).[28]

---

21 *Sporting Life*, March 1, 1886, 4.
22 *Sporting Life*, March 1, 1886, 4.
23 *Aberdeen Evening Express*, March 29, 1886, 4.
24 *Aberdeen Journal*, April 12, 1886, 5.
25 *Aberdeen Journal*, May 10, 1886, 7.
26 *Dundee Courier*, July 5, 1886, 2.
27 *Aberdeen Journal*, July 19, 1886, 2.
28 *Aberdeen Journal*, January 10, 1887, 7.

Scotland's last week-long, indoor race for male professional pedestrians was the seven day, 21-hour, contest in Aberdeen in April 1886 with a field of twenty-six, won by Cartwright of Walsall (£20) with a good total of 176 miles from local man Willie Corbett's 174 miles.[29] The women's races were still attracting decent fields of mainly local pedestriennes, but the Aberdeen race at New Year 1887 was the last to offer worthwhile prize money. The long-distance professionals put on a few challenge matches, but public interest was not enough to sustain another bout of professional pedestrianism.[30]

By the end of the 1880s the six-day era in Britain and America was played out. After a dozen years when it had been a popular and lucrative sport it had reached the end of the track. The top-class runners had achieved what was thought to be the limit of the sport – in 1888 at Madison Square Garden George Littlewood of Sheffield covered 630 miles in six days of almost continuous movement. The non-specialist audience were thought to be losing interest in the gigantism of these events. Other sports had experimented with the six-day format, swimming, cycling and even roller-skating, but could not stand against the Saturday afternoon sports of football and rugby. For the competitors, amateur athletics was still available as a sport and in Scotland in particular professional pedestrianism lived on for the sprinters, but this was not an option for the women.[31]

The last competitions at which a ghost of the great distance events was to be seen in Scotland were in the far North-East at the fishing port of Peterhead where in 1888 amateurs put on a series of 'go-as-you-please' races. Enthusiastic amateurs circled a fish-curing yard for two hours a night for three nights in pursuit of prizes such as a marble clock or a silver watch.[32] This shadow of the events of the past in its turn faded away; but the fascination with great distance recurs throughout history and can be seen perhaps resurrected in the people's marathons of the modern era.

---

[29] *Aberdeen Evening Express*, March 29, 1886, 4; April 5, 1886, 4.

[30] In September 1888 in Aberdeen Miss Jeffrey and Miss Murray walked a match over two evenings; and the unofficial world champion Joe Scott (unsuccessfully) took on a relay team of three Scottish pedestrians over six days, thirty-six hours, losing by 209 miles to 214 (*Aberdeen Evening Express*, September 10, 1888, 3; *Aberdeen Journal*, September 15, 1888, 8).

[31] David A. Jamieson, *Powderhall and Pedestrianism* (Edinburgh: W. and A.K. Johnston, 1943), provides a detailed history of the famous Powderhall sprints in Edinburgh (still extant).

[32] *Peterhead Sentinel*, May 15, 1888, 7; May 22, 1888, 1; June 8, 1888, 2.

Conclusion: Being a pedestrian

The first competitors in the six-day races had been experienced athletes. Pedestrianism in the 1870s and 1880s could still provide a precarious living. The pedestrians were not the high-minded Corinthians of late Victorian dogma; they had come up in a hard trade. The new six-day races were to them another way to exploit their abilities in the pursuit of a living wage. Tom Brown, for example, who walked 384 miles in the Glasgow match of June 1879, was not only a top class runner, but had 'considerable notoriety' as a 'circle walker' which meant that he gave exhibitions of race walking on the stage in music halls. [33] William Clarkson, a hardened Yorkshire pedestrian who competed in seven Scottish races and at least twenty down South was also a circle walker when the opportunity arose: after he had run 151 miles in the two-day, 24 hours tournament at Perth in January 1880 he appeared every night the following week at a music hall in Dundee, walking a mile around the stage (probably about a hundred circuits) in less than eight minutes.[34] Several had done solo walks of days or weeks. Pat M'Carty of Leeds, who appeared in four contests in Scotland in 1879-80, had done solo walks such as the 400 miles in five days at the York Skating Rink in 1877.[35] David Ferguson of Pollokshaws competed in eleven races in Scotland, a gruelling six of them in 1880 alone, culminating in an impressive 403 miles in sixty-five hours on a circus ring at Dundee in December.[36] George Noremac was even more prolific: he did thirteen races in 1880, ten of them in Scotland and was so successful that he went to America, had some big victories in 148-hour races and remained to die there in Philadelphia in 1922.[37] At the lower end of the scale, it was just possible to survive on sporadic small prizes. J.S. Robson from Liverpool had a career total of at least twenty-four six-day races. He had been a seaman, he was in his fifties and lived the life of a peripatetic pedestrian, often walking between races. In February 1880 he walked the 140 miles from Aberdeen to Glasgow and then walked in a six-day, twelve hours a day race.[38] He rarely won a big prize but was a crowd

---

[33] As, for example, at Blaydon in 1872, he walked three miles in under 22 minutes (*Era*, December 22, 1872, 5); *Glasgow Evening Telegraph*, April 22, 1879, 6 ('considerable notoriety').

[34] *Dundee Evening Telegraph*, January 6, 1880, 2.

[35] *York Herald*, December 3, 1877, 1.

[36] *Dundee Courier*, December 13, 1880, 2. He won £45 in prize money.

[37] *Philadelphia Inquirer*, February 18, 1922, 12.

[38] He arrived twenty minutes late for the start; in the race he made 309 miles for fourth place and a prize of £3 (*Dundee Evening Telegraph*, March 1, 1880, 2). His next (six-day) race started in Perth eight days later, and another two weeks after that in Leeds.

favourite known for his cheerful demeanour and occasionally playing popular airs on the harmonica as he walked.[39]

By their very nature, six-day races demanded full-time commitment, at least for a period. But most pedestrians had to have a job to fall back on. William Corbett, who managed to compete in at least fourteen Scottish races, was a coal heaver from Aberdeen, Joe Leith, also of Aberdeen, was a drover, Pat M'Carty was a clogger.[40] Most seemed to barely scrape a living, and a few had brushes with the law. Alexander Clark was arrested for debt on the track in the middle of a six-day match in Glasgow, bringing it to an abrupt termination[41] (it seems to have been an occupational hazard, Cartwright from Birmingham was arrested on the track in a 36-hour event at Sheffield for deserting his wife and children - he had been in the 26-hour race at Aberdeen two weeks earlier, the newspaper reports had been his downfall.[42] Joe Leith ran in the 21-hour contest at Aberdeen in April 1886 and was stabbed to death in a drunken argument at an abattoir in the same town a couple of weeks later.[43]

As with the men, many of the women who raced in Scotland were professional pedestrians and, in some cases, it is possible to follow their careers of several years in the 'walking trade', though only fragments of personal information can be recovered, not least because many of them worked under stage names. Madame Englo was a dressmaker.[44] She appeared in the first British female-only race, in Plymouth in 1879,[45] and went on to become one of the most successful female pedestrians. She walked in Scotland in the one-to-one contest with Kate Brown at Dundee in 1882, for which she earned £10 and a gold medal, and returned four times to Scotland during the 1886 revival. By then she was thirty-eight or thirty-nine years old, had been a full time professional for at least seven years (twelve by her own account) and had appeared in at least twenty-five pedestrian matches.[46] Her greatest rival, Kate Brown, was probably already a professional when she appeared in the first multi-day female event in Scotland (the six-day walk against Janet Day at Glasgow in 1879). She appeared another five times in six-day races in

[39] *The Referee*, February 29, 1880, 5.

[40] *Aberdeen Evening Express*, March 12, 1887, 3.

[41] *Edinburgh Evening News*, July 4, 1879, 2.

[42] *Sheffield and Rotherham Independent*, April 28, 1882, 4.

[43] *Aberdeen Journal*, April 1, 1886, 4; April 24, 1886, 4.

[44] *Lloyd's Weekly Newspaper*, August 17, 1884.

[45] *Western Morning News*, April 7, 1879, 1.

[46] *Edinburgh Evening News*, November 11, 1881, 4.

Scotland in a career of at least a dozen such races over seven years. The 1879 race was Janet Day's first known race (she was probably from Glasgow herself). She went on to have career of five years in England, where she walked in at least half a dozen races and several solo walks including a 1,000-mile walk in 1881.[47]

When female six-day events flourished briefly in 1886-87 these professionals were, as already mentioned, outclassed by the cohort of novice walkers from the North-East. Few details of them have survived but the most successful of them achieved an unsought notoriety. 'Miss Lorimer' was Margaret McPhee, a thirty-three year old mother of five, an Aberdeen fishwife, married to William McPhee, a scavenger.[48] She seems to have taken up pedestrianism with the February 1886 Aberdeen six day race, came second in that, won at Dundee in March, and was placed at Glasgow in May and Dundee in June, winning over £50 altogether (say £5,000 today). Her anonymity was broken on her appearance as a witness in the Aberdeen Police Court. On her return from her win at Dundee she was assaulted by her husband, who complained that he had to look after the children while she was away and did not receive a fair share of the winnings. He was convicted of assault and the couple separated soon afterwards.[49]

Whether male or female pedestrian, the indoor arena was not for the squeamish. In the big venues, such as the Agricultural Hall in London or Madison Square Garden in New York there were laps of 250 to 290 yards (six or seven to the mile) and a bark or sawdust track. But at the provincial venues the best you could hope for was a reasonably spacious hall. Concert halls, recreation halls, meeting halls, drill halls or even town halls were used or maybe a gymnasium or a warehouse. You might have a wooden track and sharp corners. But a circus ring could be worse. Cooke's and Newsome's circuses in Dundee, Aberdeen and Glasgow were used for at least a dozen of the Scottish races (they were probably semi-permanent wooden structures). Their tracks were painfully short, thirty-five to forty-five yards (up to forty-seven laps to the mile). The pedestrians learnt to cope - there is a record of Willie Smith of Paisley doing a mile in six minutes and five seconds round a circus ring track at the six day contest at Dundee in 1879 (a dizzying

---

[47] She walked the thousand miles at two miles every consecutive hour for twenty-one days on the bowling ground of a pub near Preston (*Preston Chronicle*, January 15, 1881, 3).

[48] 1881 Scotland Census, Aberdeen St. Nicholas, ED 39, page 14 ('Margaret McPhee').

[49] *Aberdeen Evening Express*, March 31, 1886, 3; May 21, 1887, 2.

thirty-five laps of fifty yards at ten seconds a lap).[50] Short tracks were also narrow – there were twelve starters on the track at Newsome's Circus in Glasgow in 1880, which was six feet wide and raised four feet above floor level.[51] Even hall tracks could be very cramped and this sometimes led to friction between exhausted pedestrians. At the Drill Hall in Perth in a twelve hours a day race in December 1879 where there were nineteen starters on a 41 yard track Clarkson and Clark came to blows and Clarkson was disqualified (he was allowed back on and at the end got a subscription from the spectators for his 'pluck').[52] At the same venue in March 1880 M'Kellan and Hill were both disqualified for fighting.[53]

---

[50] *Dundee Advertiser*, December 22, 1879, 3.

[51] *Glasgow Herald*, February 24, 1880, 7.

[52] *Dundee Courier*, January 1, 1880, 3.

[53] *Dundee Courier*, March 15, 1880, 3.

10

Military Regulations Suppressing Sports Movement: Cycling During the Great War in Occupied Belgium.

Filip Walenta

Abstract
As sports and leisure activities behind the front lines in occupied Belgium during the Great War have been rarely examined, the purpose of this study is to get a clear idea about the way sports, and especially cycling, were engaged in during this difficult period. A deeper insight is revealed into how German regulations influenced the local mobility and cycling in particular. Also, sports competitions were difficult to organize. The cycling races became local events with local athletes and the way they were structured changed significantly. The national competitions were cancelled for four long years and the functioning of the cycling federation was reduced to an absolute minimum. Nevertheless, sports competitions, including cycling races, survived in other forms due to the innovative ideas of the organizers.

Keywords: First World War; Sport; Cycling; Mobility; Belgium.

Introduction
On Sunday 28 June 1914 two events happened at the same moment: the departure of the twelfth Tour de France in Paris with a total distance of 5404 km divided over 15 stages, and the assassination of the Austrian Archduke Franz Ferdinand II and his wife Sophie Chotek by the Serbian nationalist Gavrilo Prinčip in Sarajevo, causing a snowball effect that would lead to the beginning of the First World War.

Five weeks later. on Sunday, 2 August 1914. Philippe Thys, the overall winner of the Tour de France for the second time in row, was celebrated at his arrival in the railway station in Brussels.[1] A cycling race in the velodromes of Brussels and Ghent on Monday was planned with Thys, but cancelled due to the threat of war.[2] Instead of earning extra prize money as a guest racer Philippe Thys took his luxury car to the nearby

---

[1] *Het Nieuws van den Dag*, August 2, 1914.
[2] *Het Handelsblad*, July 29, 1914; August 1, 1914; *Het Nieuws van den Dag*, August 4, 1914.

military camp and volunteered in the Belgian army.[3] At the same day Luxemburg was invaded by German troop and two days later they crossed the Belgian borders. Obviously, all sport activities were cancelled during their Westerly progression through the country. The editorial office of the leading sports newspaper *Sportwereld* wrote:

> It will not surprise anybody that today we are not able to provide any sports news or any results of cycling races. The people are sufficiently enough informed about the international complications to realize that the general attention is focused upon other things than amusement. Consequently, all cycling races in the country are cancelled.[4]

At the end of October 1914, the progression of German troop into Northern France came to a standstill, and the movement of war changed into trench warfare.

Sperrgebiet, generalgouvernement, etappengebiet, operationsgebiet and marinegebiet.

As the Western front was situated near the Belgian-French borders Belgium was consequently divided into two parts: the *Kaiserliches Deutsches Generalgouvernement Belgien* and the *Sperrgebiet.*[5] The General Government was a civil occupation authority while the *Sperrgebiet* was a military area under the command of the 4th Army. It was prohibited for civil traffic and divided into three areas: the *Marinegebiet, Operationsgebiet* and *Etappengebiet.*[6]

The *Operationsgebiet* (area of operations) was a 10 to 15 kilometres wide strip following the Western front from the North Sea towards the Suisse borders. The *Marinegebiet* near the coast that had to be secured against an eventual invasion of allied troop was also considered as an ops-area, especially the harbour of Ostend as the U-boat headquarters deployed there needed extra protection.[7]

---

[3] *Het Vlaamsche Nieuws*, November 25, 1914; *LDH*, November 28, 1918.

[4] *Sportwereld*, August 3, 1914.

[5] Sebastiaan Vandenbogaerde, *Een kijk op de administratiefrechterlijke organisatie van het Etappengebied tijdens de Eerste Wereldoorlog* (Ma. Dissertation: UGhent, 2010), 32-34.

[6] Ibid., 48.

[7] Ibid., 49.

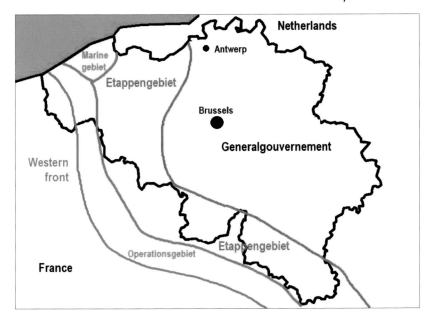

Fig. 1. Map of Belgium during WWI divided in several strategic areas.

In *Etappengebiet* we recognize the French word *étappe*. Today *étappe* is a French term for a day race in a multiple (bicycle) stage race, like the Tour de France. The place of arrival of a stage is mostly the starting point for the next stage the day after, this is why it is considered as the resting point. But originally it was a French military term, meaning 'resting point for the army' in the eighteenth century, and later in the nineteenth century 'distance between two military resting points' or the distance that an army could cover in one day. As the army could progress approximately forty to fifty kilometres per day, the *Etappengebiet* was a forty to fifty-kilometre-wide area that followed the troop in the frontal zone.

With the quasi stationary Western front almost parallel to the French borders, the whole area West of Brussels and the Southern parts of Belgium remained *Etappengebiet* during the whole war. As there was a lot of movement it was a logistical and administrative area for the supply of fresh troops, weapons, ammunition, material and vehicles, and also a resting place for fresh and returning troop with a lot of (field) hospitals for wounded soldiers.

In order to assure a smooth transition of troops, weapons and material, and to avoid sabotage, espionage or revolts, a harsh regime for the civilians was installed. Therefore, several regulations for the local population were introduced. Crossing municipal borders was forbidden without a pass, all public festivities on the street were forbidden, especially national holidays and public (sport) events in the street.[8] As a consequence, relatives and friends who lived in different villages did not see each other for four years. The only possible communication between them happened by exchange of letters. In addition, people who had fled their homes during the period of the German invasion and wanted to put their families' minds at rest wrote small announcements in newspapers.[9]

Mobility and sports
Cycling in *Operationsgebiet* en *Marinegebiet* was prohibited, especially on certain strategically important traffic lanes. In the *Etappengebiet* and *Generalgouvernement* initially cycling was prohibited as well, but later from spring 1915 it was allowed in the cities and outskirts but (as mentioned before) crossing municipal borders was forbidden. For those who had to use their bicycle and needed to cross the borders for professional reasons a special pass valid for an area of five kilometres radius was available. The pass had to be requested and renewed every fourteen days in the office of the local German headquarters.

All kind of sports and leisure events on the street were forbidden and were banned in sporting fields and gyms. As a consequence, the younger team sports gained popularity very quickly. Football, for example, was one of the sports that became popular in Belgium during the Great War due to unemployment and the restrictions on crossing municipal borders. In 1915, regular football competitions were organized again in the bigger cities Ghent, Brussels and Antwerp, but only with clubs from within the city borders, while in the suburbs and the countryside new clubs were founded at a very fast pace.

Stijn Streuvels, a Flemish naturalistic author wrote in his diary that would be published ten years after his death in 1979:

> The new phenomenon is football, the game that used to be played only by sportsmen and students. Before it was completely unknown in the countryside, but now football is played everywhere. Every village got her own club and when an appropriate field is found, the game is on.

---

[8] Sebastiaan Vandenbogaerde, *Een kijk op de administratiefrechterlijke organisatie van het Etappengebied tijdens de Eerste Wereldoorlog* (Ma. Dissertation: UGhent, 2010), 81-84
[9] *Het Volk*, April 7, 1915

and, 'Every kind of game was being played, adults would even play marbles just to kill the time'.[10]

Cycling races and athletes

In consequence of the German regulations, cycling races in the street were forbidden in the whole occupied area, except in Brussels where very occasionally a street race was allowed. These races were organized inside on home trainers and rollers during wintertime, and in velodromes during the summer, including the classic races. This was not new because in 1911 the classic Sedan-Brussels had been organized in the velodrome of Linthout near Brussels.[11] The track on the street was projected into the velodrome and all regulations were at force as during the classic races. The racers had to restore their own bicycle during any break-down and were not allowed to get help from anybody. During their 'passage in the cities' check points were organized to avoid cheating and to be sure everybody had done the complete distance. The racers had to stop and sign the participant's list or get a stamp on their jersey number. At the check point the participants could have some extra food and drinks, spare tyres and material.

Most of the bicycle races that were organized during the First World War in occupied Belgium have been forgotten for the last hundred years but these have been revealed since the start of this study. As a single event they do not have any significance at all, except for the classic races that carry a famous name. But all together they show that the sporting and cycling life was pretty much alive, and that the statement by some authors that 'cycling died a quiet death during the First World War' as we will discuss later in this chapter is based upon personal interpretation and loose ends, caused by several different reasons.

The Ghent Six Day race, for example, was until now considered to be organized for the first time in 1922. Nevertheless, this study revealed the existence of the very first edition in 1915 from Sunday 3 till Monday 11 November, around the same period of the Brussels six-day race. The race was organized over nine days, with in between three days off, divided over three velodromes in the outskirts of Ghent: Mariakerke, Gentbrugge and Evergem.[12] The duration of the day stages of the races resembled much of the six days as we know them today. Instead of the

---

[10] Stijn Streuvels, *In Oorlogstijd. Het volledige dagboek van de Eerste Wereldoorlog*, (Brugge/Nijmegen: Orion/B. Gottmer, 1979), 485.

[11] *HLN*, April 7, 1911; *Het Nieuws van den Dag*, April 8, 1911; *GVA*, April 10, 1911

[12] *De Vlaamsche Post*, October 6, 1915; *Gazet van Brussel*, October 3, 1915; *Het Volk*, October 1, 1915.

continuous six days by teams of two members the races took six hours on Sundays and four hours during weekdays due to the compulsory curfew.[13]

Fig. 2. A hundred-kilometre cycling race at the Karreveld velodrome (Brussels) on June 12, 1915.

Another forgotten cycling classic is the Tour of Flanders of 1916, organized in the Gentbrugge velodrome on Sunday, 23 July 1916 as a 125-kilometre race with four intermediate sprints after 25, 50, 75 and 100 km.[14]

According to previous sources, Karel was supposed to be the organizer of the Tour of 1915.[15] He apparently heard about the cycling race in the Brussels velodrome in June and remembered the success of the Tour of Flanders in 1914, jumped on his bike and drove to the Evergem velodrome to organize the Tour of Flanders. But, as Karel lived in Torhout, a very important garrison in the *Operationsgebiet*, he simply never could have got the permission to leave his town for such an 'insignificant' reason, and certainly not for a longer period to make all the preparations. Also, in 1916 there had to be another organizer as

[13] Regulation poster in the Ortz-Kommandatur Aalst, October 21, 1918; *Het Volk*, October 21, 1915; *De Vlaamsche Post*, February 13, 1916

[14] *Het Volk*, July 25, 1916; *Vooruit*, July 13, 1916; July 20, 1916; July 25, 1916

[15] Achiel Van Den Broeck and Berten Lafosse, *Zo was … Karel Van Wijnendaele*, (Kortrijk: Atlas, 1962), 23-25

Karel was forced to work for the construction of the airfields near his town.[16]

New-found information about cycling events in Ghent in 1916 has revealed the real organizer. According to newspaper articles some of the cycling races were organized by the magazine *Sportwereld*.[17] A small article mentioned that Leon Van Den Haute, general manager of *Sportwereld* and founder of the Tour of Flanders, lived in the centre of the city of Ghent and married his fiancée Elodie Dick on the same day of the race.[18] So it was quite clear that Van Den Haute must have been the organizer of the Tours of Flanders during the German occupation or at least must have given the permission to use the brand name.

Just like the rest of the Belgian population, cycling racers spread out over whole Europe during the First World War. The biggest number stayed in occupied Belgium and found extra jobs to survive as they mostly donated their prize money for charity purposes like war orphans, prisoners of war in Germany, etc.[19] Smuggling foodstuff and transferring espionage letters, photos and microfilms became a lucrative business for the daredevils of the cycling peloton. Among them Paul Deman, winner of the first Tour of Flanders in 1913, who did several missions until he was arrested by the Germans. After questioning and torture in the prison of Leuven he faced the death penalty but was finally rescued by the Armistice in November 1918.[20]

A lot of cyclists had joined the army and stayed for four years at the Western front, eventually being killed in action or taken as prisoners of war. Philippe Thys had brought his car and drove high rank liaison officers about from one meeting to the other. During his time off he kept on training and even succeeded in winning the cycling classics Paris-Tours and the Tour of Lombardy in 1917.[21]

Others had fled to the Netherlands after the battle of Antwerp and lived in refugee and prisoners of war camps. To kill time, they managed to build a velodrome in the Harderwijk camp and organize cycling meetings. From the camps in Holland a few even migrated to the United

---

[16] Ibid., 26

[17] *De Gentenaar*, August 17, 1915; *Le Quotidien*, September 23, 1915

[18] *Het Volk*, July 27, 1916

[19] *Het Vlaamsche Nieuws*, October 18, 1916; October 28, 1916

[20] Patrick Cornillie, *Koersen in de Groote Oorlog*, (Tielt: Lannoo NV, 2018), 108-109, 168

[21] *Gazet van Brussel*, June 29, 1918

States to compete six-day races, like Michel Debaets and Victor Linart.[22] In general they also donated half of their prize money to charity organizations in Belgium.[23]

As cycling racers were considered as adventurous acrobats some of them were recruited as pilots in the air force. Among them was Hélène Dutrieu, a former female cyclist who obtained her flying license in 1910 as the first Belgian female pilot.[24] During the war she led Red Cross ambulances and later the field hospital in Val-de-Grâce.[25] Rumours have it that although female pilots were not allowed in the French air force she did some recce flights and also participated in the air defence of Paris against zeppelin attacks, but until now no proof of this has been found.

Cycling died in 1916?
A few resources mention that the cycling movement decreased significantly from 1916. This statement is generally based upon a mixture of several facts and personal impressions. Two events at the turn of 1915 were of political nature and had a hidden but immediate effect upon the ordinary life in Belgium. King Albert I had seen the thousands of casualties caused by the mindless attacks of allied troops, only to gain a few hundred square metres and to lose them again a couple of days later. He feared that his troops would suffer the same fate and refused to bring them under the general command of the allied forces. A second reason for his refusal was that he did not want to give up the neutrality of his country. This was the official version. The unofficial reason was that in the autumn of 1915 there were high level diplomatic contacts between the close entourage of the king and the German government without the Belgian government's involvement. King Albert I thought that there would never be a victor of the war and it would be better to make a compromise peace with Germany. However, in February 1916 he rejected the German terms, broke off the negotiations and brought the Belgian troops under the general command of the allied forces after the successes at the battles near the Marne in July 1918.[26]

---

[22] *Gazet van Brussel*, July 22, 1916; *HLN*, December 1, 1918; *Het Nieuws van den Dag*, November 28, 1918

[23] Patrick Cornillie, *Koersen in de Groote Oorlog*, (Tielt: Lannoo NV, 2018), 64

[24] Ibid., 30-32

[25] Ibid., 80

[26] Els de Witte, Dirk Luyten and Alain Meynen, *Politieke geschiedenis van België: van 1830 tot heden* (Antwerpen: Manteau, 2016), 166-167

The continuous poverty of the German working class, the long duration of the war, and the status quo position of the Western front led to the emergence of war-weariness in the German cities. The increasing political response of left-wing parties put extra pressure upon the government and the military authorities in Berlin. Consequently, in the autumn of 1916 the German army responded with increasing attacks on the Western front and a harsher regime for the local population. The country was treated as a German colony, everything that could help the German troops was confiscated. Food distribution happened infrequently, and meat was rationed to only 150 grams per person per week.[27] *Zivilarbeit*, forced labour, was introduced for the unemployed locals living in the *Etappengebiet*. They were transported to Northern France near the frontal zone to work under horrible conditions. According to a study conducted by specialist-researcher Donald Buyze almost eight thousand civilians would not survive German slavery.[28] All the bicycles and rubber tyres were confiscated, except for those who needed their vehicle for professional purposes. Consequently, there was a lack of everything, bicycles and cycling material included.

Alongside these difficulties came the demolition of several velodromes. The two most important velodromes in Antwerp and Brussels were demolished because the land was bought by investors for the construction of new sports halls and fields, wooden velodromes like those in Ghent and Aalst were broken down due to increased wood prices and lack of investment. Other places saw an increase of cycling races and sports events like the Gentbrugge velodrome, while the velodrome of Garden City near Antwerp even reopened their doors in July 1915 after closing since the outbreak of the war.[29]

An important issue was the political position of the cycling union, as most of the board members were conservative nationalists. After the reconstruction, most of the velodromes started to reopen their doors during early Spring 1915. At the same time, an important meeting was organized in the head office of the cycling union LVB-BWB in Brussels. Out of nationalistic persuasion and as a symbolic rebellion against the German occupation, they decided that all cycling races had to be cancelled. In other sports like football the unions had similar ideas. Of course, this decision resulted in a lot of turmoil. Several parties feared

---

[27] Giselle Nath, *Stad in de storm. Arbeidersvrouwen en het hongerjaar 1916.* (Gent: Handelingen der Maatschappij voor Geschiedenis en Oudheidkunde te Gent, 2011), 213.

[28] Mail by Donald Buyze, April 10, 2019.

[29] *Echo de la Presse*, July 25, 1915.

losing their biggest source of revenue, the velodromes by loss of entrance fees and the athletes by loss of prize money, while, in addition, the union requested all members (organizers and athletes) to pay their license fee for 1915 for administrative purposes. Finally, union members budged on their decisions on the condition that a part of the entrance fees would be donated to charity. In addition, they had to admit that due to the mobility restrictions the union could not send any representatives to weekly events. Consequently, the cycling union could not function as before and, although cycling races kept ongoing as local events, nationally organized competitions came to a standstill.

We also must consider the fact that most of this part of the study is based upon sports articles in newspapers. Next to the fact that the press is not always the most reliable resource we know that the existing newspapers were censured, and that collaborative newspapers were sponsored by the Germans. Sport events and sports articles in the newspapers were tolerated because they were harmless for the regime, it kept the locals quiet and gave them the impression that normal life went on. But as paper became too expensive most of the newspapers were forced to decrease in size, and others simply disappeared. Consequently, writing space was reserved for more important issues and sports articles were the first to decrease or to disappear as well. The decreasing sports articles gave the wrong impression that the sports activities were disappearing. Also, Stijn Streuvels mentioned in his book that 'For those who have no passport cycling is prohibited – thus also the races – Tour of Belgium etc.[30] Streuvels simply could not have known that cycling had died because there were no velodromes in the neighbourhood where he lived, and he also could not cross municipally borders. So, his statement is clearly based upon personal interpretation and hearsay.

Conclusions
German restrictions did have a significant negative impact upon personal mobility, sports and leisure activities and the transfer of sports information. Federations and unions could not function anymore, and they lost their overall objective to lead and assist their local associations, the clubs, competitions and events. Consequently, cycling competition was reduced to local events with the participation of local athletes. Indeed, from 1916 cycling races saw a downturn, or at least gave that impression, but did certainly not disappear. Sports events just went on during the Great War, including cycling races. As with ordinary life,

---

[30] Stijn Streuvels, *In Oorlogstijd. Het volledige dagboek van de Eerste Wereldoorlog*, (Brugge/Nijmegen: Orion/B. Gottmer, 1979), 484

they were replaced, or the concept changed, some velodromes were demolished while others reopened their doors.

Fig. 3. The Groote Scheldeprijs of September 29, 1918 organized in the Garden City velodrome of Wilrijk near Antwerp.

Even when the German army was forced to retreat in the autumn of 1918 and the Western front moved further Eastwards into Belgium, sports events just went on. On Sunday 29 September in the velodrome of Garden City the oldest Belgian classic, the Groote Scheldeprijs, was organized over 175 kilometres and in the velodrome of Gentbrugge several sporting events like athletic and cycling races, and football matches, were played halfway through October 1918. Another point of view was found in the press after the Armistice of November 11, 1918:

> Concerning cycling, motor and car driving, the three sports have done a great job during the War at all levels: as a post service, supply of food and ammunition, etc. In brief, the War did not kill the sports as sometimes is asserted but has even caused the expansion of it. We therefore want to inform our readers that we, just like before the war, will continue to provide articles of all sporting events.[31]

---

[31] *Het Nieuws van de Dag,* November 27, 1918.